the

WEDDING OFFICIANT'S GUIDE

the

WEDDING OFFICIANT'S GUIDE

How to **WRITE & CONDUCT** *a Perfect Ceremony*

Lisa Francesca

CHRONICLE BOOKS
SAN FRANCISCO

Page 133 constitutes a continuation of the copyright page.

Library of Congress Cataloging-in-Publication Data:
Francesca, Lisa.
 The wedding officiant's guide : how to write and conduct a
perfect ceremony / by Lisa Francesca.
   pages cm
ISBN 978-1-4521-1901-4
 Includes bibliographical references and index.
 1. Weddings—United States—Planning. 2. Weddings—
Planning. I. Title.

HQ745.F73 2014
392.5—dc23

                        2013046733

Manufactured in China

Designed by Hillary Caudle
Typesetting by Sean McCormick

10 9 8 7 6 5 4 3 2 1

Chronicle Books LLC
680 Second Street
San Francisco, California 94107
www.chroniclebooks.com

for Peggy

PREFACE

for the BRIDE or GROOM
scanning this book

DEAR NEWLY ENGAGED,

You've asked your cousin, or your sister, or your best friend from high school to marry the two of you. What can you expect from them between now and your wedding day? And what should you watch out for, since you have just asked an amateur, rather than a professional, to perform this most important task?

You should expect your officiant to:

- Take the necessary steps to ensure that he or she can legally officiate at your wedding.
- Interview you, maybe more than once. You'll discuss your preferences for the ceremony and talk about the things that make you a unique couple.
- Send you a draft or two of the ceremony so you can make any changes.
- Coach you in getting your wedding license within the right time frame.
- Be at the rehearsal and know how to steer the guests and the wedding party in the right direction.
- Arrive early to both the rehearsal and the wedding.

During the ceremony, everything the officiant does should be to support you during your transformational moments. Officiants dress soberly, stand calmly, and speak clearly, allowing for pauses and natural moments of tenderness or humor. Your officiant should not pull any surprises or make inappropriate jokes.

After the ceremony, your officiant should secure signatures from your witnesses and file the license with your county. Overall, your officiant should be reliable, organized, and discreet. Your happiness must be the paramount goal in her or his mind.

This book will let your officiant know exactly what you're expecting from her or him, and how to do it all. You might also enjoy browsing through part two of the book for wedding-ceremony options, rituals, and readings before you hand it over to your newbie officiant. 🌿

INTRODUCTION

HOW I CAME TO PERFORM WEDDINGS

"Sweetie, this is your old man," began the recorded message. "I've gone ahead and ordained you online through the Universal Life Church. If you have questions, contact Brother Daniel in Modesto. And I'd like you to shadow me at rehearsal on Saturday; it's in wine country." Click.

I sank slowly into the chair I'd borrowed, at the desk I'd built from a cheap kit. My nine-year-old daughter and I had just moved into a tiny apartment in a city where we didn't know anyone, and I had just been laid off from a copywriting job at a technology company. Me, a minister?

I'd always wanted to go to seminary. I'd read books and pieces of world scriptures and philosophies, even taken courses in prayer and meditation. But between raising a family and working, I had no time to commit to several years of intensive study. Also, I was raised in a family that included practitioners of different faiths, so if I did find the time, I wasn't sure which school of thought would accept my untraditional interfaith ideas.

Now my dad, Hank Basayne, was inviting me to join his business. Since his peers had ordained him as a Humanist minister in 1968, he had performed nearly eleven hundred weddings, memorials, and other ceremonies in the greater San Francisco Bay Area. Health issues were beginning to multiply and slow him down. He needed a backup. And I needed a job.

Ordination online was free. I spent some money on the credential, which I later framed. And I bought a little card to stick on the dashboard of my car showing that a minister is on the premises. No one in ten years has asked to see my credential, but the little dashboard card has been helpful for parking at weddings.

Shadowing my father, I met couples of every description and brides in every stage of pre-wedding anxiety. There were fainting grooms and missing licenses, and separated parents forcing themselves to act courteously after years of feuding. I saw dogs bearing rings, and little boy ring bearers who vomited, and rings that flew off their ring pillows. Windy gusts tore at long bridal veils, and bees lurked in lawns. There were also masses of flowers, happy tears, gorgeous dresses, musicians, favors, doves, and comic asides.

Dad looked handsome in his black robe or his suit and tie, smelling of Old Spice. It fascinated me that after performing hundreds of weddings, he still looked forward to each one with keen enjoyment, anticipating another adventure. "You may recite a certain passage or hear a certain reading scores of times," he reminded me, "but don't forget that your wedding couple is hearing it for the first time. That's why it never gets old, and why you should never recite anything mechanically." Dad likewise warned me not to over-rehearse my lines, so that when the time came, my script offered me some of the sense of wonder and surprise that it gave the guests.

One day he gave me his second-best robe, a black one with a hook closure at the neck. It hung heavily and made me feel authoritative.

Rather than follow in my father's Humanist footsteps, I decided I would be an interfaith minister. That means I can perform both spiritual and secular or civil ceremonies—I'll explain more about those in chapter one. My particular interest lay in weddings that combined different faiths and cultural traditions. A Japanese groom and a Jewish bride. A Filipina bride and a Midwestern Methodist groom. Ordinarily, couples who belong to the same church tend to get married in their church. My constituents would be the unchurched, as well as people whose churches would not accept their spouse. Or their earlier divorce. Or their decision to marry in a park surrounded by redwoods.

In addition to our love of weddings, Dad and I shared a passion for writing. A few months before he died, I sat with him at his dining-room table overlooking San Francisco Bay, discussing ideas. "Lisa," he suggested, "by now you know a lot about weddings. Why don't you write a book about what you know?" The more I thought about it, the more excited I felt about writing a guidebook for you, the new officiant.

Aside from giving you the permission and the tools to have fun while doing something unusual and important, I'm also writing this to raise the bar of officiating in general. I have winced too often when an officiant, professional or not, forgot something as critical as the groom's name. I've cringed at an officiant's awkward jokes, or long-winded story about himself.

Perhaps you are fresh from seminary, ready to begin a long career of wedding couples. This book is for you, too; just skip the ordination section. Whether you'll ever conduct only one wedding, or go on to preside over many more ceremonies, you want to give the couple your closest attention and best effort.

WHAT MAKES A GREAT OFFICIANT

As an officiant, you'll be using the skills and traits in the following list. If you feel rusty in a particular area, you may want to brush up.

- **PUBLIC SPEAKING.** You can speak in public; in fact, you rather enjoy it—especially from a script you don't have to memorize.
- **LISTENING.** You know how to listen carefully. This will help you get to know what the wedding couple really wants. And on stage, during the ceremony, you must be able to listen for any unexpected things that crop up so you can handle them.
- **RESOURCEFULNESS.** You can write a draft of the wedding ceremony, and if your couple asks for optional readings or ceremony rituals that aren't in this book, you know how to research online, or in your library.
- **ORGANIZATION.** You'll create a file with your notes about the wedding. You'll print your script and put it in a binder. You'll receive the marriage license before the wedding and keep it safe with the script. After the wedding, you'll make a copy of the license for your files and then mail the original license to the right address.
- **RELIABILITY.** You show up on time, which means early.
- **WILLINGNESS.** Patience. Kindness. Humor.
- **FLEXIBILITY.** You are able to roll with any punches and ad lib as needed.

Once you know that you have the qualities you'll need, you've taken the first step toward feeling confident in your new role as an officiant. ✤

part one

HOW TO PERFORM
A WEDDING

*I*n the first part of this book, you'll find a systematic description of the entire officiating process from the moment a couple asks you to perform their wedding to the moment you file their license. You'll learn how to work with the marriage license, how to interview the couple to create the most appropriate wedding ceremony for them, how to handle rehearsal, and how to perform every step of the wedding.

Throughout the book, you'll also read stories from new officiants about their experiences and lessons learned from their weddings. And you'll find practical tips from well-respected wedding planners on how best to manage the sequence of events on the big day.

chapter one

YOUR ROLE

Someone you know has asked you to perform his or her wedding. Maybe you are a friend or a relative. Perhaps it's because of your regal, stately bearing or your musical voice. Or maybe you are doing them a serious favor by keeping their wedding bills down and under budget. Whatever the reason, they've invited you, and you've accepted the honor and challenge. Now what?

The process of performing a wedding, while simpler than neurosurgery, does involve some care and organization on your part. You will have to become either deputized or ordained (unless you are conducting a ceremony that doesn't require licenses; more about those later in this chapter). You'll have to perform the wedding and say specific things at the right time, and you must mail a signed, completed marriage license for the wedding to be legal. And the legalities are just the bare bones.

A wedding, on its most basic level, is about a couple making a contract and sealing it with public words. As they say those words, their community witnesses the act and acknowledges that a transformation has taken place. When the rehearsal and the big day arrive, many people—parents, guests, musicians, and other vendors—will look to you for calm, graceful leadership. After all is said and done, you want a wedding couple to feel pleased with the ceremony you've created and happy with your delivery of the ceremony. It's a big deal.

It's also a generous form of service to your friends and family. It will give you a unique perspective on weddings, and create good, shared memories within your community. As an officiant, you'll learn an unusual new skill and have a chance to speak deep, meaningful words in public. And you don't even need to memorize your lines. You'll work within the safety of reading a script, knowing that the spotlight is trained on the couple, not on you. Finally, you'll wield an interesting form of power: the couple can't be married without you and your expertise. You advise them about when and how to get their marriage license. You'll explain the milestones of the ceremony ahead of time, helping them to feel relaxed and confident. You are entrusted to be the calm person at the core of the swirling activities and variables of a wedding. You will modestly usher them across the threshold from singlehood to married life.

WHAT YOU'LL CALL YOURSELF

Your role allows you to call yourself one of three things: an officiant, a celebrant, or a minister (if you're ordained). Or you can just say you've been deputized for the day. Most people aren't very familiar with the term "celebrant," so be prepared for a blank look. "Officiant" has better traction because it is somewhat related, in people's minds, with official, judge, and notary. But it can also sound a little stuffy.

A person with a religion or a spiritual practice might feel comfortable calling himself or herself a minister. After all, he or she is ministering to the couple, and performing clerical, administrative tasks. If you do call yourself a minister, be sure that the couple is comfortable with that designation. One couple, whose families were upset that the wedding would take place outside their family church, asked me to call myself a celebrant. They felt that word would be less emotionally charged for their parents.

Why should you decide what to call yourself? At the rehearsal and wedding, you will want to identify yourself right away to the wedding coordinator, the families, the musicians, and the photographers, so that they can take direction from you as needed and not confuse you with the caterer or an assistant. You will also need to identify yourself on the wedding license, so give the matter a little thought before moving on.

─── WHAT YOU'LL DO ───

By taking on this role of officiant, celebrant, or minister, you are agreeing to:

1. Ensure that you are legally authorized to perform the wedding ceremony.

2. Meet with the wedding couple to determine what they want from their ceremony.

3. Advise them on how to obtain their marriage license.

4. Draft a wedding ceremony based on your interview with the couple and other research you have done, and let them review and edit the ceremony.

5. Accompany them to the rehearsal, and manage the rehearsal if necessary.

6. Fill out your part of the license.

7. Marry the couple on their wedding day.

8. Acquire the witness signatures on the license, and make a copy of the completed license for your folder.

9. File the original license (by mail or in person) with the appropriate county clerk.

10. Plan to provide an acceptable substitute officiant if, for any reason, you cannot perform the ceremony.

Performing all these tasks requires an understanding of the importance and solemnity of this legal, community-oriented activity. At the same time, it can be a lot of fun.

HOW LEGAL OFFICIATING WORKS

An officiant is a person who performs, conducts, solemnizes, officiates at, or presides over a service or ceremony such as marriage, burial, or baby welcoming/baptism. In the United States, each state has laws that grant authority or entitlement to individuals so they can solemnize marriages within its borders. The term "officiant" includes justices of the peace, celebrants, marriage commissioners, ministers of established religions (including Native American medicine men or women), notaries (once they register), and other people empowered by law to conduct legally binding private ceremonies. Officiants may be ordained by any denomination as members of their clergy, or by secular, Humanist, or interfaith religious bodies. (Contrary to popular myth, a ship's captain does not have the legal right to perform a wedding at sea simply by right of his or her captainship. The captain who does perform weddings must also be a judge, a justice of the peace, a minister, or a notary public.)

But what if you do not hold any of these roles? In some states, such as Massachusetts, Vermont, and California, you can be deputized by a county clerk, which lasts as briefly as a single day. Otherwise, consider becoming ordained by one of several online ministries. Once you are ordained, you can officiate at weddings for the rest of your life.

DEPUTY OR ORDAINED MINISTER?

Once you have committed to conducting the wedding, ask the couple if they are seeking a civil (also called secular or nonreligious) wedding or if they will want some spiritual or religious elements in the script. A deputy, having been deputized by the state, can perform only secular weddings and cannot use religious words in the ceremony, period. A person who is ordained by a church (including online churches) can perform either secular or spiritual weddings.

Becoming deputized involves a trip to the county clerk's office for perhaps an hour. Ordaining yourself online can take minutes. You would want to do either of these actions to become an officiant right away. In the next few sections, we'll take a closer look at deputization and ordination.

BECOMING DEPUTIZED

In Massachusetts, it's called a one-day marriage designation. In Vermont, you can become a temporary officiant for the sixty-day duration of the wedding license. In California, you become a deputized commissioner of civil ceremony for a day. These guidelines from San Francisco County will give you a good idea of what to expect:

- Deputization will be granted on a San Francisco County–issued marriage license only. A photocopy of the marriage license must be presented at time of deputization.
- Marriage ceremony must be performed in California.
- Person must be at least eighteen years old.
- Person is not required to be a California resident.
- Person must be fluent in the English language.
- Person will be required to take the oath of office swearing/affirming to support and defend the Constitution of the United States and the Constitution of the State of California.
- Person must appear in person in the Office of the County Clerk with valid legal photo identification.

- **Religious wording and references are not allowed** during the ceremony (emphasis mine).
- As of 2013, the fee was $128, payable to SF County Clerk.

Your county or state may not allow deputization. Check your online state or county clerk's website, on the marriage page, to see if and how you can become a deputy. If your area won't deputize you, go ahead with the online ordination; you can still conduct a civil/secular wedding if that's your intent.

A NEW OFFICIANT SPEAKS
I WAS DEPUTIZED

Andy Altman-Ohr, SAN FRANCISCO, CALIFORNIA

My cousin asked me to perform his wedding. I said yes, and we made plans to get me deputized for the day. We met at City Hall at eight A.M. He showed up with his wedding license and the administrative fee (thanks, Cousin). I had to fill out some documents, and then the clerk entered the information into the computer and gave me a "test" license. The process took about forty-five minutes. I had to raise my hand and promise to uphold my role as deputy, and this was only good for one wedding on one day. I couldn't charge a fee, not that I wanted to. Also, because deputization was a city/county thing, I wasn't allowed to use any religious wording during the ceremony. Instead of saying we had gathered to join the couple together in *holy matrimony*, I would have to say *solemn matrimony*.

—— BECOMING ORDAINED ——

You may freely obtain ordination from one of many online churches. Ordinations given by any church or religious organization are federally protected by the religious nonestablishment clause of the First Amendment: "Congress shall make no law respecting the establishment of religion, or prohibiting the free exercise thereof." You do not have to pay for an ordination, but you can choose to purchase a certificate for a nominal fee. You enter your name and address into their official database record of ordained clergy; it takes a few minutes.

By far, the most popular online ordination is through the Universal Life Church (ULC), which has ordained close to eighteen million people since it opened in Modesto, California, in 1962. According to its website, "The ULC ordains individuals without question as to beliefs, free of charge. This is the official authorization and entitlement granted to all ULC ministers. The church's authorization and entitlement is granted for life."

There are offshoots of ULC, and with the confusion in names comes some bad blood between the different entities. The two best ULC alternatives for getting free ordination are www.ulc.net (the founding church in Modesto, California), and www.ulc.org (a reputable offshoot in Seattle). Two other options are the American Marriage Ministries, a not-for-profit church established in Washington state (www.theamm.org), and the Church of Spiritual Humanism (www.spiritualhumanism.org), which claims more than one hundred thousand members.

A special word: Your ordination should be free or at nominal cost. One site, such as First Nation Church, might ask you for an annual donation; another may demand a tuition fee of $150. These are not free ordinations!

LEARN THE LOCAL REQUIREMENTS FOR OFFICIANTS

Seattle-based American Marriage Ministries keeps an online library where you can find the legal requirements to officiate in the state where the couple will marry. For example, you'll find here that you can be deputized in California, but not in Connecticut. In some states, your act of online ordination is enough, but in others (such as Hawaii, Connecticut, West Virginia, and Minnesota), you must also register your credential and possibly even file a letter of good standing with the county. In Ohio, for example, county clerks always require ordination credentials with handwritten signatures on them. Laws for Nevada and for New York City are more complex than for other areas and may change. It's a good rule of thumb to triangulate any information you get on the web. Check these sites, and follow up with a phone call to your county:

- www.theamm.org/marriage-laws
- www.themonastery.org/tools/wedding_laws

If you plan to marry the couple in a different state from where you live, be sure to check *that* state's legal requirements for officiating right away so you have time to fill out any needed paperwork. In the state of Nevada, where weddings provide lucrative livings for many officiants, your out-of-state permission might take three months or longer to obtain.

These are precautions to satisfy the law, should any questions arise about the marriage license that you'll file after the wedding. If you make an error about the location of the wedding (such as naming the wrong county), you can remedy that by filling out another license and paying a fee, but there is no easy remedy when a wedding is declared invalid because the officiant was not credentialed.

WHEN ONLINE ORDINATION IS NOT ACCEPTED

As of the writing of this book, most states and counties accept the Universal Life Church's online ordination. Even though Pennsylvania and Virginia generally reject ULC ordination, one county within each state *will* accept it: Bucks County, Pennsylvania, and Spotsylvania County, Virginia. If you live in the rare county that does not recognize online ordination, but your couple still wants you to officiate at their wedding, perhaps the simplest thing is to get their marriage license from a neighboring county that recognizes the ordination. Your couple can still be married anywhere in that state.

MARRYING OUTSIDE THE UNITED STATES

If your sister in the Midwest wants a destination wedding in Hawaii, you can ordain yourself, fly out there, and legally officiate. But if she wants to get married in Fiji or the Caribbean, Canada or Europe, or Africa and beyond, she should choose an officiant who is local to that destination to ensure that the marriage is legal. For example, Canadian law requires and allows a temporary registration certificate to be issued through the Registrar General of the Province in order to solemnize marriages, but each Registrar General gets to decide whether the online credentials are acceptable. Another large headache that wedding couples may encounter is the residency requirements of that country. And the pre-wedding process may take several interviews over a number of weeks. In Spain, for example, authorities may take up to forty-five days to approve a marriage application.

In any country, an American bride and groom will need to produce birth certificates and proof that they are each eligible to be married (that is, not already married to someone else). Furthermore, many countries require having an apostille (an authentication of signatures that is affixed to a document) in order to accept the necessary papers.

A WEDDING PLANNER'S PERSPECTIVE

NINETY PERCENT OF MY COUPLES MARRY BEFORE THEIR DESTINATION WEDDINGS

Alison Hotchkiss,

OWNER OF

Alison Events Planning and Design, SAN FRANCISCO, CALIFORNIA

AUTHOR OF

Destination Wedding Planner:
The Ultimate Guide to Planning a Wedding from Afar

Every country has different legal issues. In some, you can arrive and marry tomorrow; in others, you have to live there for a month first and have blood tests. It's critical to understand the requirements of your location, and some of them can seem overwhelming.

A bride who wanted to marry in Scotland had to apply for the license ninety days ahead, then physically be there for thirty days ahead, and have three sessions with a state marriage counselor. Another couple in Harbor Island, the Bahamas, had to sit for a three-hour interview. And other unforeseen issues can complicate your life. After one wedding in Costa Rica, the local office lost the paperwork! So that couple wasn't legally married. You can bypass all of this.

I highly recommend going to the city hall where you live and making it legal there. Then make your destination wedding all about the ceremony and the party.

Also, all documents brought from the United States should be translated into the destination country's language.

Your sister might choose instead to tie the knot legally at home first, in which case you can fly to the romantic destination right along with her and conduct the ceremony of her dreams without stepping on local laws.

If the legal aspects have already been taken care of, you can move on to the rest of this book to create and conduct an inspired wedding.

TYPES OF WEDDING CEREMONIES

The wedding ceremony you perform will fall into one of four categories, based on what the couple prefers. What if you lean toward one category while the couple leans toward another? You will have to consult your internal barometer to see how far you can step out of your comfort zone. One evangelist I know doesn't feel right conducting any weddings that are not Christian. Another friend is an avowed atheist, but feels fine talking about the beauty of nature, which is where his spiritual wedded friends feel most connected to their source. I enjoy working with religious elements such as blessings and scriptural readings, if couples request them. I also enjoy civil ceremonies.

THE CIVIL OR SECULAR CEREMONY

The word *secular* pertains to worldly things or to things that are not regarded as religious, spiritual, or sacred. Surveys conducted by the Pew Research Center for the People and the Press show that the number of U.S. adults who say they have no religion increased from 15 percent of the population in 2007 to nearly 20 percent five years later.

The word *civil* relates to the state or its citizenry. In weddings, the terms *secular* and *civil* are pretty much the same. In either case, you will not mention God in any form, nor give a blessing. The couple will not want scriptural readings, but readings can range from romantic to humorous to philosophical. Your remarks can include thoughts about community, family, work, passions and values shared by the couple, and love. If you are deputized for the wedding day, this is the wedding you will perform.

THE SPIRITUAL CEREMONY

"Spiritual" encompasses a broad category; the bride and groom may find their spiritual sustenance in the natural world, or in the works of certain spiritual leaders and teachers, or from the spirits of their ancestors. A spiritual couple might share variations of the Christian, Jewish, or Muslim faiths. They may follow Buddhism, Hinduism, Taoism, the Baha'i faith, Shinto, Zoroastrianism, or Sikhism. They could call themselves New Agers, Spiritualists, Unitarian Universalists, Deists, Wiccans, Pagans, or Druids. They may follow Native American traditions, or Santería, or Rastafari.

If *deputized* for the wedding, you have agreed with the state that you will not make remarks that include *God, holy, blessed,* etc. When you know that your couple wants a spiritual, religious, or interfaith wedding, things will go more smoothly if you ordain yourself online.

Ordained, you have options throughout the ceremony to add notes of spirituality. You can describe why the couple chose the location of their wedding if it has a spiritual aspect. Where appropriate, you can pause for either a moment of silence or a moment of prayer. You may be asked to bring God into the ceremony by asking Him to bless the couple, or you can ask the community to bless the couple. The same is true for blessing the rings.

You could say, "We are gathered here in the sight (or presence) of God," and add to your pronouncement that the couple has exchanged their vows "before God and this company." They might ask for prayers, blessings, and scriptural readings that have meaning for them.

THE INTERFAITH OR INTERCULTURAL CEREMONY

I love interfaith and intercultural ceremonies. The combined rituals surprise and please the assembled families and guests. I once officiated at a wedding in which a Chinese Buddhist bride married a Jewish groom.

They married under a chuppah after a traditional tea ceremony, and their parents recited blessings over them in both Chinese and Hebrew. Another wedding included a typical humorous Persian call-and-response ritual to determine if the bride was ready to marry, and ended with a mariachi recessional in deference to the groom's Mexican heritage.

An interfaith wedding may take a little research on your part to be able to suggest rituals or readings that have meaning for the wedding couple. Or they might already know what rituals they want, and your research will allow you to perform them correctly.

THE RELIGIOUS CEREMONY

Unless you are a priest or minister of a particular religion, you will be least likely to be called upon to officiate at this kind of wedding. People who have close bonds with their churches tend to go to that church to be married. I have, however, married deeply religious couples who, because of a divorce in their past or a lifestyle choice, could not be married in their beloved church. Only a Catholic priest can celebrate a Catholic mass and discuss the Catholic life ahead for the couple, but if you share an alignment of religious values with a Catholic couple and marry them outside the church, you can pray with them, bless them, make the sign of the cross, and use scriptural readings. Leave the church things to the church, but feel confident that blessings and prayers may be freely shared by all.

Outside of a church, weddings—even religious ones—can be performed anywhere: in a Japanese garden, on an estate lawn, in a vineyard or on a beach, in a restaurant, a wedding hall, or in one's home.

CEREMONIES THAT DON'T REQUIRE LICENSES

The following ceremonies do not require licenses, and they are not considered legal marriages. You don't need to be ordained or deputized to perform them. With the legal aspects removed, use the rest of this book to create an amazing and memorable ceremony for the couple, and you can completely ignore Chapter Seven: After the Ceremony.

- **HANDFASTING CEREMONIES.** Handfasting is an old (pre-medieval) betrothal ceremony of tying a length of cord or ribbon around the joined hands of two people as they make promises to each other. Historically found in Celtic, Norse, and African traditions, the ritual is also currently popular in Wiccan weddings. While handfasting can be one ritual in a legal wedding, in itself it does not constitute a legal wedding.
- **RENEWALS OF VOWS**, since the couple has already been legally wedded.
- **COMMITMENT CEREMONIES** or same-sex weddings that take place in states that do not yet recognize same-sex marriages.

A NEW OFFICIANT SPEAKS

TRIANGULATE YOUR INFORMATION

Chris Reimer, ST. LOUIS, MISSOURI

I made sure with several people that what I was doing would be legal, that I was being ordained by the right group (www.ulc .org), and I even called the city of St. Louis. They said I was fine as long as I was ordained by a church and the wedding took place on Missouri soil. Then I even called a friend in the mayor's office! And the couple appreciated that I did due diligence on their behalf.

RESEARCH WEDDING CEREMONIES, RITUALS, AND READINGS

Now that you have been deputized or ordained, your next step will be to plan an afternoon or two of research. Part one of this book shows you step by step how to perform the wedding, and part two is filled with rituals, readings, and optional texts you can use as you create the ceremony. There are so many potential variations on the elements of weddings that it is worth your time to peruse a library or bookstore. There are books on technique and even historical precedent: Why will the bride stand to your right, and in which weddings is she on your left? (You'll find the answer on pages 68 to 69.) New wedding books appear annually, so the wedding shelves of retail and second-hand bookstores will offer different perspectives. Wedding websites are also useful sources of even more rituals, customs, and options (see Further Reading, page 128, for some of my go-to sites). Grab your pad of paper or laptop and take notes.

Having acquired some familiarity with traditions and some good ideas, you are now ready to sit down with the bride and the groom and find out what *they* envision for the ceremony.

A NEW OFFICIANT SPEAKS

MY BROTHER, THE GROOM, KNEW WHAT HE WANTED

John Pennick, SAN JOSE, CALIFORNIA

I reviewed several books and got detailed instructions from my brother Mike and his fiancée, Connie, on how and what they wanted. We did a lot of planning ahead of time. They planned everything, including my part of the ceremony script. Their wedding took place on a San Diego beach on a beautiful June day. During the ceremony, a group of seagulls became a part of the wedding and squawked and squawked. We laughed.

I'd tell a first-time officiant to relax and have fun.

THE AMATEUR WHO ACTS LIKE A PROFESSIONAL

As an amateur officiant, you probably know the couple, or one of them, better than any hired officiant could. But having sincerity and better familiarity with the couple is not enough. Here are some of the most common arguments against using amateur officiants. Do the opposite to act like a professional.

He bailed out on me or arrived too late.

Have a back-up plan. You and the couple should work together to keep another officiant in the wings, either hired or not, in case of illness or accident. While the eventuality of an emergency is slim, you don't want the consequences to ruin the couple's wedding day.

She shared the ceremony with us at the last minute and we were not happy with it.

The next few chapters will help you to interview your couple and draft the ceremony with them so that they are happy with it before you even rehearse.

He fainted/said something rude/acted silly/got drunk and out of hand at the reception.

Just don't. We revisit this in chapters four and five.

After she married us, we learned her ordination wasn't considered binding in our county. She should have registered with the county first!

Learn the legal requirements of your wedding ceremony in your state. If the wedding is taking place in a different state, be vigilant about checking *that* state's requirements.

My amateur officiant forgot to get the witness signatures on the license, so we are not yet officially married.

Read on, and you will easily avoid this nightmare scenario.

chapter two

INTERVIEWING THE WEDDING COUPLE

When you know the reasons for the overall structure of the wedding, you'll be able to explain the various elements of a ceremony to the couple.

THE ESSENCE OF A WEDDING

The opening, the vows, and the closing are the essential parts of any wedding structure. Legally, all you need to create a wedding is the couple's declaration of intent to marry each other, and your pronouncement that they are married. You can just have these and nothing else. Either of the following two ceremonies from *Weddings: The Magic of Creating Your Own Ceremony*, by Henry S. Basayne and Linda R. Janowitz, Ph.D., will meet the basic minimum requirements of law in most localities:

Minimum: The officiant marries the couple

YOU: Do you, Elaine, take George to be your husband?

BRIDE: I do.

YOU: Do you, George, take Elaine to be your wife?

GROOM: I do.

YOU: By virtue of the authority vested in me by the state of (state), I now pronounce you husband and wife.

Minimum: The couple marries each other

GROOM: I, Daniel, take you, Rochelle, to be my wife. Let this ring be a symbol of my vow.

BRIDE: I, Rochelle, take you, Daniel, to be my husband. Let this ring be a symbol of my vow.

YOU: Inasmuch as you have exchanged the vows of marriage, according to the laws of the state of (state), I now pronounce you husband and wife.

While minimal weddings are expedient, most couples will want to add more to the ceremony. Traditional weddings incorporate an additional level of ritual that might include your own brief remarks about marriage (known as the *celebrant's address*) and an exchange of rings. You can further enrich the wedding ceremony with poetic readings, music, additional rituals, and family participation.

LISTEN TO THE WEDDING COUPLE

Plan to sit down with the bride and groom in a relaxed atmosphere for an hour or two during your first meeting, perhaps at their home or a quiet café. If they have posted a website about their wedding, take a look at it. During your interview, you'll guide the couple through the elements of a wedding, stopping at each juncture so they can choose additions that are most meaningful to them. Bring your notebook or laptop so you can make notes as you walk them through the elements of the ceremony. Don't be in a hurry. Invite the couple's questions, and let them take as much time as they need while making these important joint decisions about what their wedding will include. They may want to get back to you with answers they can't provide right away.

Your part is all about listening carefully. They may expect to write the draft and control the ceremony, or they may want you to handle most of it. Be open to either possibility. One partner may want to include an element that the other may not want. Often one person is comfortable speaking in front of the crowd while the other person is not. Use your intuition and diplomacy to make the wedding comfortable for both of them. It's likely that they will not know what they want for every single stop along the decision tree. That's okay—draw a little square next to that item and move on. You can check the box when it's been decided.

A BRIDE'S STORY

WE CHOSE HIS SISTER TO OFFICIATE, AND THEN WE COULD RELAX

Allison Kalsched, MAPLEWOOD, NEW JERSEY

When Jon and I decided to get married, one of our biggest concerns was who would perform the ceremony. Neither of us has any religious affiliation, and our independence is something we value highly. When we found out that Jon's stepsister, Lisa, was ordained and willing to perform our wedding, we were so excited. At our first meeting, any anxieties we had about our choice of an amateur were immediately relieved. Lisa's caring attention and sincere interest in who we were and what kind of ceremony we wanted exactly matched our hopes and expectations.

CHECKLIST: QUESTIONS THAT YIELD THE BEST INFORMATION

Before discussing the elements of the ceremony itself, ask these questions to draw out background information that will help you to manage the logistics of the rehearsal and wedding.

TIMING

- What time of day is the wedding?
- When is rehearsal: The day/night before? What time? Where will it be held? *I encourage a rehearsal, just so everyone gets to know where to stand and what to do.*

VENUE AND GUESTS

- What is the name and address of the venue? Phone number?
- If it is outdoors, is there a Plan B for weather?
- How many guests are expected? *If they do not want any guests, discuss whether they want a public or confidential marriage license (see the next section about confidential licenses).*
- If more than seventy guests are invited, will there be a microphone?

CONTACT INFORMATION

- If someone is helping coordinate this, what is his/her name? Phone number?
- What are the preferred e-mail addresses (for the ceremony drafts) and cell-phone numbers (for last-minute coordination)?

FAMILY

- Note each person's birth date and birthplace. Ask: Are you planning to keep or change your last name? Have you been married before, and if so, when was that marriage dissolved? *Why does this matter? If marriages were terminated within the past six months, the couple may have to bring their divorce papers with them as they apply for their wedding license.*

- Ask the couple to name any grandparents who will be attending. Name parents who are attending, and any divorces or remarriages that might be relevant. Name attending brothers or sisters, and any other family members in the wedding party (a cousin, sister-in-law, etc.). *This gives you names of key players so that at rehearsal and on the wedding day, you'll know who is who. You can introduce yourself to them and congratulate them. This also helps to uncover any family dynamics you should be careful about, such as divorces, feuds, or eccentricities.*

- Have the families already met? What is the comfort level between the families? *Again, family dynamics.*

WEDDING PARTY

- Names of the maid/matron of honor, bride's attendants, best man, the other groomsmen, flower girl, ring bearer. *Knowing these first names will come in handy when you line everyone up during rehearsal. If the flower carriers and ring bearers are under the age of five (or if they are pets), note that they are unpredictable and should be accompanied down the aisle by a beloved adult, preferably a parent.*

- *Ask this next question privately, as the bride may not want the groom to know what she is wearing.* Bride, will you be wearing a veil? If so, at what point would you like to have the veil lifted, and would you like to do that yourself or have the groom do it?

- What is the expected attire? A suit? A minister's robe? Is there a wedding color palette to try to follow? *There may be a color scheme. If the couple says, "Wear anything you want," what they mean is, "Show up dressed nicely." If they wear flip-flops to a beach wedding, you can too.*

—— LICENSE AND WITNESSES ——

- Does the couple know how to get their wedding license? *If they do not, review with them the next section about the license and the opportunity to change one or both last names.*

- Names of Witness One, Witness Two. *You'll need at least one witness, and no more than two. Many couples choose the best man and the maid of honor to be witnesses. You can choose anyone over the age of eighteen, even the parents. Just make sure they have been designated ahead of time.*

- After the license is filed, will the couple want a certified copy from the county? *For name changes or for people born outside the country, it can be valuable.*

—— ABOUT THE BRIDE AND GROOM ——

These questions call forth thoughtful responses:

- How long have you known each other? How did you meet? What are some things you feel passionately about? What are some of your favorite activities together? Do you have pets? What kind, how many, names? *The answers to this section can help you construct your remarks. If they met in a unique way, share the same values, or overcame some obstacles, you can weave a few lines about that into your script.*

The same is true for the questions that follow:

- Bride, what does Groom bring to the table that will contribute to the success of this marriage? What are some other things that you like about him?

- Groom, what does Bride bring to the table that will contribute to the success of this marriage? What are some other things that you like about her?

CEREMONY DETAILS

Final questions for the couple:

- How long do you want the ceremony to be? *Wedding ceremonies tend to last between twenty and thirty-five minutes. Too much longer, and guests may grow uncomfortable in their seats; if shorter than fifteen minutes, they'll be left wondering what happened.*

- What tone do you want: Secular, spiritual, religious? Should I use the words *God, bless, prayer*? Remember, if you have been deputized, you are limited to secular speech.

- Bride, will you be accompanied down the aisle? Should I ask who presents you?

- When I open the ceremony, would you like me to acknowledge anyone who is missing? Who is unable to travel, or who is deceased?

- Are there rituals you have in mind, or ones you have seen that you would like to use? *If they can't think of anything, use your judgment. You might want to recommend something from part two of this book based on what you know about the couple.*

- Do you have a reading or two already in mind? If not, and you have a friend or relative who would be a great reader, would you like me to find a piece that is classical, romantic, funny, or scriptural? *While it is up to them to communicate with their reader, you might end up handing a copy of the reading to that person. The wedding couple might prefer to have a cherished guest sing or play music rather than read.*

- Do you want to write your own vows, or would you rather repeat classic vows after me?

- Would you like to share brief letters of appreciation to each other before the vows?

- Do you want to say anything while exchanging the rings?

- Do you want a final blessing or reading before I pronounce youmarried?

Now it is your turn to give them some important information.

MARRIAGE LICENSES AND CHANGING NAMES

The license is a legal document obtained by the couple before the wedding that allows them to marry and authorizes you to marry them. This is the paper that you and the witnesses will sign, and you will file within ten days after the wedding. Remember, you cannot conduct a legal marriage ceremony without a valid marriage license.

There is no federal law regarding domestic relations, so each state creates its own form for use with the recording of marriages. In other words, the format of the marriage license in your state may vary. In general, the certification of the marriage is usually recorded on the marriage license.

The marrying couple will visit their city hall or their town or county courthouse together before the wedding, bringing legal identification and money to pay the marriage license fee. It could be the county in which they reside, or they might choose a county in the state in which they plan to marry. If the couple chooses to marry in a state other than the one where they live, they should find out about residency requirements (how long they must be in the county before they can apply to marry). For example, a New York couple could apply for a license in San Francisco, because there is no residency requirement in California, and they can then get married in any county of California. Visit the websites for the counties that you are considering and read the marriage information carefully; there may be variations to the general rule.

The license is valid for only a certain amount of time (see page 41 for length of validity in your state), so make a note of the date when the window of opportunity opens. Encourage the couple to make that visit *at least* two weeks before the wedding, when their lives are not quite as hectic as they will be closer to the wedding day. Some counties offer appointments you can schedule online, and applications that can be downloaded. There are many variables from state to state regarding the license, so learn what is required to get married in your area. The quickest way to start the process is to find your county's website online.

At the bottom of the license there may be lines allowing the couple to register a change of name. This ends up being a rather expensive thing to change later on, so make sure the couple has some time to think about who, if anyone, will change names. One can take the other's, there can be varying degrees of adding on and hyphenating names, both could take a new name, or each could keep the old one.

Although the requirements for a marriage license may vary from state to state, the Full Faith and Credit Clause of the United States Constitution mandates that a marriage in one state must be recognized as valid by every other state. States have taken conflicting views on recognizing same-sex marriages performed in other states, but the trend appears to be moving toward recognition. In a landmark ruling in 2013, John Arthur of Cincinnati, Ohio, dying of Lou Gehrig's disease, won the right to be listed as married on his death certificate and to have his partner of more than twenty years listed as his surviving spouse. The couple had originally married in Maryland, and the Ohio judge ruled their marriage legal in the state of Ohio.

After the wedding, and after you file the license, will your wedded pair want a *certified copy* of the license? Generally, the answer is yes. If one or both of them plan to change their last name, or if one (or both) of them were born outside of the United States, they will need to present a certified copy during an important transaction such as updating a driver's license, Social Security information, or passport information. When the couple applies for the license, they also receive, or can ask for, an application for a certified copy. Encourage them to keep that application in a prominent place so they don't forget about it, and to apply for their certified copy about eight weeks after their marriage. The application fee can range from $1.25 to $15.

WEDDING LICENSES
and their
EXPIRATION DATES

The varying periods of wedding-license validity across the United States reflect the diverse ways in which various states have evolved to serve their marrying citizens. South Dakota's period is the shortest at twenty days.

Alabama, Colorado, Delaware, Hawaii, Kentucky, Louisiana, Missouri, Oklahoma, Tennessee, Texas, Utah, and Wisconsin share a thirty-day period. Michigan is the only state with a thirty-three-day period.

Arkansas, Florida, Illinois, Indiana, Massachusetts, New York, North Carolina, North Dakota, Ohio, Oregon, Pennsylvania, Vermont, Virginia, West Virginia, and Washington will allow a couple to marry within sixty days of getting their license. Connecticut stretches the period to sixty-five days.

Alaska, California, Maine, New Hampshire, and Rhode Island expire in ninety days. Montana's license expires in 180 days. But Iowa, Kansas, Maryland, Minnesota, and New Jersey offer six-month licenses. Arizona, Nebraska, Nevada, New Mexico, and Wyoming give a whole year before the marriage license expires. In Georgia, Idaho, Mississippi, South Carolina, and Washington D.C., the license never expires.

Find out more about marriage laws at www.usmarriagelaws.com or marriage.about.com. Marriage laws change, so confirm your most current state laws by contacting your county by phone or online.

THE PUBLIC LICENSE

About ninety-five weddings out of a hundred require a simple public license. A public license will be signed by the couple (at the clerk's office), you (after the wedding), and at least one, and no more than two, witnesses to the wedding over the age of eighteen. If a couple gets a public license in one county, they can be married in any other county in that state. When they want to access their license, either one of them can go to the county office, or they can request a certified copy by mail. Their wedding will be on public record at the county recorder's office.

THE RARE CONFIDENTIAL LICENSE

A confidential marriage license protects all the personal information on a marriage license from public view. There will be *no* witnesses for a confidential license, and the marriage record will be sealed as soon as it enters the county clerk's office. A confidential license may be desired if your couple lives together and people don't know that they are not already married. For example, some couples with grown children have chosen a confidential license to keep those children from ever knowing that they were born when their parents were not legally married. Celebrities also might use this license to keep their marriage information private.

Or the wedding pair might feel strongly that they don't want anyone, not even you, to hear their vows. In that case, you'd be present, but out of earshot as they exchange vows, and you will sign and file their confidential license.

A confidential license requires that the wedding take place in the same county from which the license is issued. The couple can still apply for and receive a certified copy of the license. After that, only with a court order or a notarized application by either spouse can anyone obtain a copy of the information.

CHANGING LAST NAMES

The bride may intend to change or hyphenate her last name, and some grooms change theirs. The couple may even decide to take a completely new name together. Essentially, anyone changing a last name will first indicate the change on the marriage license at the county clerk's office.

Now that you have interviewed your couple, you are ready to put all the information you gathered into a draft. It will be an easy task when you use the milestones in the next chapter.

A NEW OFFICIANT SPEAKS

LISTEN TO THE COUPLE AND DO YOUR RESEARCH

Andy Altman-Ohr, SAN FRANCISCO, CALIFORNIA

We met for brunch a few weeks before and talked for an hour and a half. I also combed their wedding website and e-mailed questions to them. They offered a basic framework for me to follow, and they chose the rituals they wanted, including exchanging garlands, crushing a glass at the end, and lighting a memorial candle for the bride's father. There were also a lot of Sri Lankan names that I practiced and rewrote phonetically so I could say them properly.

A NEW OFFICIANT SPEAKS

THE COUPLE AND I CREATED A LIVE-TWEETED WEDDING

Chris Reimer, ST. LOUIS, MISSOURI

My friend's officiant had just cancelled, so my friend and his fiancée asked me to become an ordained minister and marry them. The couple had found each other on Twitter, which they both turned to in times of insomnia. I had worked with this friend at a social-media ad agency, so it was natural that they'd invite their friends to a live-tweeted wedding.

I wrote the ceremony in a Google document, and my couple reviewed it with me. We made text changes while conferring online and quickly nailed down the ceremony.

On the morning of the wedding, the groom took the wedding script and broke it down into tweets using a unique hashtag for the occasion. He loaded up my account on his laptop, and then a site facilitator used his laptop to cut, paste, and tweet the wedding as it progressed. She did a phenomenal job! Later on, the tweets were Storified.

It's healthy to be a little paranoid about all the details; be vigilant about everything. Get there early, and if you use technology, bring a paper copy. Just in case.

chapter three

DRAFTING THE CEREMONY

With the information gathered from your interview with the couple, you can begin a draft of your ceremony. This chapter describes in detail the milestones of a wedding ceremony so you can decide whether an element works for your draft.

In brief, they are:

- Processional/Entrance
- Welcome
- Opening blessing/ Moment of silence
- The bond of family
- Rituals and/or readings
- Words of advice to the couple
- Dedication or notes of appreciation

- Declaration of intent
- Exchange of vows
- Exchange of rings
- Closing blessing
- Pronouncement of marriage
- The kiss
- Recessional
- Announcing a moment for the bride and groom

You do not need all of the milestones, and your wedding ceremony might not even take as much time as it takes you to read about all the elements. If you jot down a paragraph or two of notes for each milestone you wish to incorporate, in roughly the same sequence as I present here, you will have a solid wedding script that you can enhance and polish.

MILESTONES OF THE WEDDING CEREMONY

It can be helpful to view the wedding ceremony as an hourglass. Starting at the top of the glass, everyone gathers together from different places. You narrow the focus for guests by explaining why they are gathered, and each successive ritual serves to sharpen that focus until you reach the vows, the center of the hourglass. After that, the actions of exchanging rings and a kiss, and your pronouncement all serve to create the opening, the bottom of the hourglass, for the newly transformed couple to return to their community. Let's consider these milestones one by one.

PROCESSIONAL/ENTRANCE

In most cases, you lead the procession, followed by the groom and his groomsmen. Some grooms prefer to come in after the groomsmen. Once you are all standing up front, grandparents and parents who are not giving away the bride are ushered to their seats. Then, usually one at a time, the bridesmaids enter, followed by flower children and ring bearer. Start your draft by listing the names of the wedding party in the order in which they will enter. The order might change after rehearsal, but still, it is a comfort to the wedding couple to be able to see all the names of their wedding party on the draft. After the last flower child, note to yourself to say, "Please rise for the bride."

The final person to enter is the bride, who may be escorted by one or both parents, a relative, a friend, or may simply arrive by herself. The groom generally steps forward to meet her and escort her to the altar. Historically, the bride was brought by her father all the way to the groom, but because this was a form of property exchange, we can happily do away with that custom. Likewise, it has been traditional to ask, "Who gives this woman, (bride's name), to be married?" Some brides will want this, and the standard response is for her father to say, "I do," or "Her mother and I do." In keeping with our more feminist age, you could alternatively ask, "How does this woman, (bride's name), come to her marriage?" The response would be, from a family member or friend, "Freely, and of her own choosing." In your draft, jot down whichever exchange the couple prefers. Note to yourself in bold letters to say to the audience, "Please be seated."

A NEW OFFICIANT SPEAKS

THEY ALL JUST STOOD THERE

Andy Altman-Ohr, SAN FRANCISCO, CALIFORNIA

It was happening. The string quartet. The processional. The bride and groom on stage in front of me. I started my welcome speech. Something didn't seem right. What? What?!

I had never told the guests, who had risen for the bride, that they could sit down.

"My bad," I said. "Please be seated." I think I detected both smiles and faint annoyance from the guests as they seated themselves.

WELCOME

The welcome is also known as the *convocation*, from the Latin meaning "a calling together." Most people are familiar with the words, "We are gathered here today," but there are many other ways to start a wedding, for instance, "Let us make a wedding!" or "Welcome, everyone, to the wedding of (name) and (name)." You establish the story of why everyone is here and what will take place. You might want to say why the bride and groom chose this place, and this day or season, to get married. Or add a line about their love for each other, and what made them decide to marry. Write the welcoming paragraph, a total of five or six sentences, using what you've gathered from your interview.

OPENING BLESSING/MOMENT OF SILENCE

After the welcome, the officiant often makes an *invocation*, calling forth a spiritual presence to the wedding, or setting this time apart from other times. If the wedding is religious, you might use a prayer. If not, a moment of silence can help people bring all of their attention to the ceremony. You could say, "Let's just take a moment to remember why we are here, and what each of us wishes for this couple."

THE BOND OF FAMILY

After the moment of silence or prayer, the couple might like you to express appreciation on their behalf to everyone who traveled so far to be there, and to acknowledge anyone absent who is important to the couple—a relative who is ill, or in the armed forces, or could not travel, or a beloved deceased relative or friend. Make a note of the names the couple gives you, or use general terms like "their grandparents." You can follow that with a statement such as, "They are with us now, in our hearts." The couple may decide to light a candle or place a flower on the altar to honor the absent family member. Make a note of that.

Then you can say a word about the importance of the family and friends who are assembled. You could talk about the fact that two families are coming together, perhaps with different histories and different customs and traditions. It is said that the process of a wedding "strengthens the family tree."

RITUALS AND/OR READINGS

From this point on in the wedding ceremony, several opportunities present themselves for rituals or readings. A ritual is how a couple symbolically demonstrates the start of their new life together. They might pour two glasses of wine into a single glass, or use two lit candles to light a larger candle, or make their vows with their wrists bound together with a length of ribbon. As you and the couple talk about including a ritual or two, it might help to review the rituals described in chapter eight.

For a reading, a wedding guest or a member of the wedding party stands and reads a short piece that is wise or romantic, thought-provoking, spiritual, or funny. A reading will flavor the tone of your ceremony. Does your couple want a scriptural or poetic tone? Ancient or modern? Or do they prefer the light wisdom of Dr. Seuss? If your wedding combines two faiths or cultures, does the couple want each culture represented by a reading? These are questions you can raise, questions they will want to think about.

Some couples invite their guests to stand and speak spontaneous or scripted good wishes for the marriage. While this can work, you run the risk that someone will have an awful lot to say; perhaps this is why most people opt to save the spontaneous expression for the reception, when everyone is seated and food and drink are flowing.

The couple may have readings already in mind, but if not, you can find a good assortment of readings in chapter nine of this book, as well as in other wedding books and online. The reader should first and foremost be someone who enjoys speaking in front of a crowd and who has a voice that can carry. Choosing a reader is a good way to delegate a wedding task to someone the couple wants to involve somehow, perhaps someone not already in the wedding party.

Natural pauses, such as after you mention the bond of family, lend themselves to ritual and readings. You will not want to choose many—that would make the wedding too long and tedious. A typical twenty-five-minute ceremony might involve two shorter readings and a ritual. As you help the couple choose their readings or rituals, take the environment into account; a candle ritual can be disastrous in an outdoor ceremony if the wind kicks up, or just as scary in a small space with a poufy bridal dress.

Send an e-mail to your couple with some options for rituals and readings from this book or others.

WORDS OF ADVICE TO THE COUPLE

Typically called "the celebrant's address," this is your opportunity to make brief remarks about what marriage means. If the couple is young, your message will be different than if they are mature. If children of one or both of the couple are involved, you can talk about what this marriage will mean for them. Ask questions that elicit this kind of important information.

It's important to remember that this paragraph or two that you write is about marriage and the couple. It is not necessarily the time to bring in a story about when you knew the groom, or your own marriage. Keep your focus.

DEDICATION OR NOTES OF APPRECIATION

Before vows are exchanged, you can confirm with the couple that they are ready to be married. You can ask, "Of all the people you have met, you have found each other. Are you ready to be married?" The couple could say, "Yes," or "We are." This exchange of words builds a frame around the vows to come, which is why it dedicates the next portion.

Traditionally, this is when the priest or minister says, "If anyone knows why these two should not be married, speak now or forever hold your peace." In the days before technology, this question might reveal if one of the couple were still married to someone else. Nowadays, the process of getting a license pretty much preempts that possibility, so hardly anyone asks.

In a religious ceremony, you could offer a prayer (a consecration) at this point to separate the sacred vows, which lie immediately ahead, from everything that has come before. In a nonreligious ceremony, you can say, "Now, as (name) and (name) prepare to exchange their vows, let's all take a moment to remember our own promises."

One popular way of dedicating this moment is to ask the bride and groom to read a short piece to each other, perhaps a love letter or a note of appreciation that they have written beforehand. Before the wedding, you will have printed out these short pieces so no one has to struggle with memorization. This reciprocal reading of letters only works if the bride and groom both are up for it. If one of them hates public speaking, it won't work. But if they want to do this, give them this guideline: Seven to ten lines is great, and more than a single-spaced page of exclamations is probably too long.

DECLARATION OF INTENT

In order that everyone may hear the couple's declaration of intent to marry, you can ask the traditional questions: "Do you, (groom), take (bride) to be your wedded wife, to love, honor, and cherish, to have and to hold? Will you stay with her for better or worse, for richer or for poorer, in sickness and in health, until death parts you?" The groom can answer, "I do," and you'll follow with the same question for the bride.

That last phrase about death can be rewritten as, "As long as you both shall live," or, very popularly, "From this day forward."

If the bride or groom feels shy about public speaking, all they have to say is "I do." But if they want to say more, they can make vows.

EXCHANGE OF VOWS

Vows are spoken promises, and the most common delivery is for both bride and groom to repeat what you say line by line:

"I (groom), take you (bride), to be my wedded wife,

To love, honor, and cherish, to have and to hold . . ." and so on.

Vows can be traditional or modern. A statement of appreciation, as described in the preceding section, can be used as a vow if it includes the promise (in so many words) that one will love, honor, and cherish the other.

It sounds best when one person's vows are roughly the same length and weight as the other. I once did a wedding on Angel Island for a couple who had met at a Burning Man festival. They had courted by tweeting for more than a year before marrying. Is it any wonder that they made sure their vows were exactly 140 characters long?

The couple may want to write their own vows. Reassure them if they fear that their phrases are not articulate or eloquent enough. Vows do not have to be complicated.

EXCHANGE OF RINGS

Rings are a visual reminder of the vows, a statement both to the couple and to everyone else that they are married. You can choose to begin the ring ceremony without fanfare, saying something like, "Rings become an enduring symbol of the exchange of vows that we have witnessed here today." Or maybe the couple would like to add a little to your script about the meaning behind the rings. They might want you to explain why they designed or made the rings a certain way, why the bride will wear her grandmother's ring, or what they have inscribed on them.

In spiritual and religious weddings, you can bless the rings by saying either "God bless these rings" or "We bless these rings."

The exchange of rings also gives the bride and groom a chance to voice their commitment by saying, "With this ring, I thee wed," or the modern, "With this ring, I join my life to yours." The exchange of rings can also be used as a place for the couple to exchange their vows, each saying his or her vow as he/she slips the ring on the other's finger. Here are more options:

"As this ring encircles your finger, may you be surrounded by love."

"With this ring I pledge to you all that I am."

"Just as this ring has no end, neither shall my love for you."

At this point, make sure that everything your couple chose for vows and rings is reflected in your draft.

CLOSING BLESSING

Unless the wedding ceremony is secular, the conclusion of the ring exchange is a good time to call a blessing, also known as the *benediction* (good saying), upon the couple. You may bless them, or parents or other guests can stand and say brief blessings, offered in the moment or thoughtfully written beforehand, to send them off together in their new life.

A religious ceremony includes a prayer here, such as the Lord's Prayer in Christian weddings. A ritual such as jumping the broom or breaking a glass can fit well here or after the next section.

PRONOUNCEMENT OF MARRIAGE

The couple might prefer that you say, "By the authority vested in me by the State of (State), I now pronounce (groom and bride) to be husband and wife," or something like, "Having exchanged their vows and rings in our presence, (groom and bride) have in fact pronounced themselves husband and wife." You can alternatively pronounce them "a married couple." There is no need to linger over this part of the ceremony, because everybody, bride and groom included, are eager to get on to . . .

THE KISS

You can have fun here, by inviting the bride to kiss her groom, or saying, "You may now kiss each other for the first time—as a married couple." The most traditional, of course, is inviting the groom to kiss (or salute) his bride.

THE RECESSIONAL

After the kiss, the bride can turn to her maid of honor to retrieve her bouquet, and then take her husband's hand or arm as they step into their new life together. They will be followed by members of the wedding party, the family in the front rows, and you.

ANNOUNCING A MOMENT FOR THE BRIDE AND GROOM

Encourage the bride and groom to walk away from the crowd right after the ceremony, sit for ten or fifteen minutes, and even have a snack together before they return and mingle with their guests. After all, they have just changed their lives in a big way, and they face a long evening as party hosts. In Jewish weddings, this custom is called *yichud*, or seclusion. You can set the guests' expectations about this. Offer to stay behind with the wedding party and announce from the altar or stage, "The newlyweds will spend a few minutes together. Let's follow the wedding party up to the refreshments, and the couple will join us shortly." A wedding photographer's schedule for family photographs might necessitate you adjusting your announcement to keep certain family members close, something like, "Will the members of both immediate families stay here with me? The rest of you, please enjoy the cocktails in the next room."

CREATE YOUR DRAFT

If you have been making notes for yourself, it's time to sketch out your draft so the couple will be able to follow along with the events. At the top of the first page, write "The wedding of" and the wedding couple's full names. Under that, write the day of the week, the date, and the year. Under that, write the place (either the town or the name of the actual location, if it is a park or an estate) where they are marrying, as well as the county and state.

List the sequence of your wedding elements, and then use your notes and the resources in this book to fill in the parts. I prefer to write out the words that I will say in phrases that are not very long. The result is that my wedding script looks somewhat like a long poem, about six or seven pages. Another person might just want to make a list of bullet points if they feel comfortable talking about each one. For the final touch on your draft, weave in the personal information you know about the couple, such as the things they like to do together. Leave yourself enough time to create the draft. Depending on your writing style, creating a draft could take a couple of hours, or a couple of days. But don't obsess—have fun with it.

When you send your draft of the ceremony to the couple, enclose a cover note that reminds them to bring their marriage license to the rehearsal. Give them time to make changes, and plan on one or two rounds of revisions before they sign off.

TELL COORDINATORS AND FLORISTS ABOUT THE PROPS

When the bride and groom are happy with the draft, it will make a great difference to the wedding coordinator if you send a copy of the final version, pointing out the props you might need for your rituals. If your couple wants to give a rose to each of their mothers, the florist can prep those roses ahead of time. No coordinator? Then it's up to you and the couple to be responsible for props well in advance of the wedding.

CONDUCTING A SAME-SEX WEDDING

Same-sex marriage is legal in more than a dozen countries, while both the Supreme Court and public opinion are steadily bringing same-sex weddings into the mainstream of U.S. culture. During this long-term, worldwide movement against marriage discrimination, a same-sex wedding will inherently contain a thread of historic precedence. The politics of using a newly acquired right to marry could add emotional pressure on the couple as they make decisions about their ceremony. If you are planning a same-sex wedding ceremony and

FUNNY,
BUT NOT A JOKER

As you draft the ceremony and begin to visualize yourself at the wedding, plan to be warm and friendly, and to put the couple and their guests at ease. If something awkward occurs, you can even use humor to preempt tension and get the ceremony back on track. When my father once performed a wedding on top of Mount Tamalpais, an overeager groomsman had tied the two rings to the ring pillow with fishing line. He had used square knots. From a pocket somewhere in his robe, Dad produced his pocketknife and cut the line, whereupon both rings flew into the air and immediately disappeared into the tall summer grass that surrounded the couple. This was not a time to get flustered. Dad smiled and said, "We're having a bit of technical difficulty, and we could use some volunteers with good eyesight to hunt for the rings." Everyone chuckled. Less than ten minutes later, both rings were found and the ceremony proceeded.

At the same time, if you are a comedian, be warned: This is not time to write in your routine. The wedding ceremony is not about you, and your remarks made simply for laughs may not be appreciated. Does the couple want the ceremony to be hilarious? Use your best judgment, but know that intentional slapstick at a wedding ceremony might be remembered by the guests long afterward as, "Wow, those vampire teeth were really inappropriate."

you sense that your couple are feeling stressed or overwhelmed, give them room to tease out and talk through any issues. Encourage them to incorporate elements that they enjoy and to let go of expectations. They are not obligated to manage the feelings belonging to family or guests who have not yet attended a same-sex wedding. One couple voiced a wish that they could elope to avoid some difficult family politics, but in the end they decided that their wedding day itself might foster positive changes, and it did.

The same-sex wedding you conduct will proceed very much like any other wedding. The couple you work with can choose, at traditional junctures in the ceremony, whether they will change a tradition or even use it at all. Your brides or grooms might wish to each be accompanied during the processional, or walk in together, or walk in alone to join each other at the altar.

The city of San Francisco has printed new marriage licenses. Instead of "Bride" and "Groom," the revised form holds signature spaces for "Party A" and "Party B." You can use this principle when you decide with the couple who will stand on your right and who will stand on your left. The person on your left (traditionally the groom) can initiate the vows and the ring exchanges—or not. One bride said to me after reviewing her draft, "Why does my partner always get to speak first and do the ritual first? Is it because she's taller?" Together we adjusted the script so she could perform the first action of the ritual.

They might take each other as a lawfully wedded wives, husbands, spouses, partners, or companions. You might pronounce them as a married couple. Find out what the couple feels comfortable with, and follow their lead.

CONDUCTING A PRIVATE CEREMONY OR AN ELOPEMENT

You might be asked to perform a private ceremony. Because there are no witnesses, the wedding license must be a confidential, not public, license (see "The Rare Confidential License," page 42). Here is a sample:

YOU: Let us make a wedding! Louise and Doug, today you enter the next phase of your growing relationship by declaring your love for each other and your intention to live together for the rest of your lives. Our laws and customs require that we publicly acknowledge this new legal union, but you two need neither ceremony nor process of law to tell you what you already know. No one, neither the state, nor a religion, nor I can create this marriage. Only the two of you can do that. Doug, Louise, treat yourselves and each other with respect, and remind yourselves often of what brought you together. You may now recite your vows to each other. *You walk out of earshot and wait to be called back. The couple exchanges their vows. You return.*

Please affirm to me: Have you freely chosen to combine your lives in marriage, to live together in love and honesty, cherishing, comforting, and honoring each other?

COUPLE: We have.

YOU: Doug, Louise, in expressing your private affirmations, you have pronounced yourselves husband and wife. May you find comfort, security, and vitality with each other. This private ceremony is now completed.

A very small wedding might have just the couple and a witness. They will apply for the common public marriage license because it will be witnessed. You can use any of the words you have seen so far; it is unlikely that the couple will want anything elaborate.

An eloping couple will rarely even think about having a witness. But if there is no witness, the bride and groom must first get a confidential license. That means that the wedding must take place in the same county in which the license was issued, and down the line, they will both need to be present in order to access that license. If the couple wants to elope in a different county, ask if they or you can bring a witness, thus allowing them to get a public marriage license. My husband once accompanied me to a beach where I married a couple just after sunrise. He witnessed the license and took a few commemorative photos of them with their camera.

A NEW OFFICIANT SPEAKS

I PERFORMED A CATHOLIC-BUDDHIST WEDDING

Kate Evans, SAN JOSE, CALIFORNIA

My friend from school asked me to officiate at her wedding. She and the groom are Californian, and their parents are from Vietnam—one family traditional Catholics, the other traditional Buddhists. The bride wanted poetry, not religious texts, to be central to her wedding ceremony.

I got ordained online. It was free, and I got an identifying card for $20. The bride drafted the ceremony, and I gave suggestions, feedback, and several poems to choose from. We went through five drafts before the bride declared it final. I rehearsed my part aloud a few times before the rehearsal. At the actual rehearsal, I read the whole ceremony right through. The wedding planner suggested I slow my voice down, which I did. The bride was super-organized and gave me the marriage license at the rehearsal dinner.

The couple did a tea ceremony in Vietnamese before our wedding ceremony. The bride's family gave the groom a necklace, a family heirloom, which he placed on the bride's neck.

I took a few deep breaths so I could hear the words we were saying with my heart, and speak from a centered place. I think my delivery was good. I choked up at the end, as I pronounced them husband and wife. I was a little embarrassed, but I was feeling the strength of that moment. Later, the couple wrote me a note saying it was very sweet that I was moved.

For the newbie, I'd say, "Do it!" It's fun. Listen to the couple.

chapter four

COUNTDOWN TO REHEARSAL

THE COUPLE APPLIES FOR THE WEDDING LICENSE

Find out the expiration date for marriage licenses in your couple's state, or the state in which they will marry, and make a note to remind the engaged couple when the window has opened for them to get a license. Earlier is better. Ask them to send you a note to let you know it's done. Again, you and your couple can find out more about marriage laws at www.usmarriagelaws.com or marriage.about.com.

A WEEK BEFORE THE WEDDING

Practice your lines. Review your draft and read parts of your script in front of a mirror. It is so much easier and more fun to perform when you have rehearsed a couple of times in the mirror first. The most common mistakes for new speakers are speaking too fast and keeping their heads down. Practice speaking at a slightly slower-than-natural pace. Remember that to pause occasionally not only helps you think, but also lets the effect of your words sink in with your audience. Be familiar enough with a few parts of your script that you can look up at the couple and the audience from time to time, not reading every word.

Check your appearance. Be sure to dress neatly even if you plan to wear a robe. Whether it's a black-tie occasion or a festive beach wedding, dressing appropriately shows your respect for the couple and for the wedding. Trim your hair and fingernails, and shine your shoes. Assume that you will be in full sight—all of you, from head to toe.

PRINT AND BIND YOUR SCRIPT AND READINGS

I once arrived at a rehearsal with an unstapled script. It was a windy day and my fluttering and flying pages contributed confusion to the proceedings. Avoid that by taking a little time to print and bind your script and whatever readings you'll use.

You can choose your method of binding. Some ministers already have their scripts bound into little books; those weddings are rarely tailored to the couple. I have also seen an officiant carry his wedding on index cards—nice and compact, unless you encounter a strong wind at the altar. Yet another officiant had a half-size binder, again nice and small, but it had seven rings, and an odd size.

I recommend the slimmest possible three-ring binder in white or black, depending on the season, what you'll wear, and the bride's preferred colors. I once agreed to bring a brown binder, which took some hunting. Plan to hold your binder from the beginning of the wedding through to the end, since you will most likely stand without any sort of lectern between you and the couple. If you must perform a wine ceremony or a handfasting, there should be a small table by you holding those props, and you can rest your binder there as you perform the ritual.

In this binder, you can hold seven to ten transparent plastic sleeves from an office-supply store. Then, into the sleeves, slip the script pages back to back so that as you leaf through it reads just like a book, with text on both sides of the page.

Plastic sleeves can be helpful for several reasons. Since there are nearly always small changes to the script during rehearsal, you can just pull the individual page out from the sleeve, make the change, and slip it back. The plastic also eliminates the rustle of turning pages, and makes it easy to turn them without getting two at a time, or having to lick your finger—something you wouldn't want the couple or their guests to observe. Plastic sleeves have also been lifesavers during a rainy or windy outdoor wedding. Everything remains in place and easy to see. And finally, after your ceremony, it will be simple for you to lift the script pages out and place them into a souvenir folder for the couple, without any holes punched in them.

Most binders have a pocket on both the inside front and back covers. Plan to slip the directions to your venue in the front, as well as your notes about the wedding. The back pocket can hold the license, a black (non-leaky) pen, and perhaps a folded handkerchief in case someone gets teary. Voilà, your binder has turned into a complete wedding kit.

THE READINGS AND/OR VOWS NEED PRINTING TOO

Some members of the wedding party will want to bring their own vows or readings, and they will show them to you: a tiny, folded-up scrap of paper taken out of his pocket or even her bra. Let them do what they want to do, but offer at rehearsal to make a copy of the vows or reading for them (in a good-sized font, perhaps even in a plastic sleeve, or, if they are short vows, on an index card), which you can hand them at the appropriate moment.

Readings and vows in their plastic sleeves or on index cards can all fit in your binder until you hand them to the right people at the right time.

THE SOUVENIR COPY

Would you like to leave behind an unexpected, thoughtful wedding gift? Bring a two-pocket folder, either white or a color that goes with the wedding. Write the couple's names on the front. After the wedding ceremony, and after you've had the license signed, remove your wedding script (with all its changes—it's a historical record, after all) from your binder and place the whole thing in the inner back pocket of the new folder. If you were given a souvenir license, slip that one (filled out by the witnesses) into the inner front pocket. If there is no souvenir license, perhaps you have vows or readings, or a note from you. Whatever you include in it, this folder will be a beautiful reminder of the event. Leave it on their wedding gift table.

Your shopping list at the office supply store might thus include some of the following:

- Binder for your script
- Plastic sleeves for your script pages and readings/vows
- Index cards (4" x 6" are preferable)
- Two-pocket folder for the souvenir copy
- Hole punch if you decide not to use plastic sleeves

ONE DAY BEFORE REHEARSAL

If they have not given the license to you already, remind the couple to bring it to the rehearsal. You could also suggest they tell their wedding party that the partying will begin right after the rehearsal, not before. This little detail will ensure a much smoother and speedier rehearsal. And as for *you* and drinking, it is not advisable to drink before the rehearsal or the wedding. You'll be glad you restrained yourself.

PREPARE FOR THE REHEARSAL

For both the rehearsal and the wedding, you'll want to show up early to review logistics and do a sound check. So *in advance*, get detailed directions to the site, check the level in your gas tank, your tire pressure, and the water and coolant in your car, and listen to the traffic reports. In other words, do everything you can to ensure that you will arrive early. Special note: Be aware that Friday-afternoon traffic usually sucks! Leave an hour earlier than you normally would.

Dress well that day, though not in what you will wear to the wedding. Bring your script and a pen and expect to make a couple of changes as you figure things out during rehearsal, such as the order of the wedding processional. Bring comfortable shoes and a sweater or jacket. Other useful items to pack for both rehearsal and the wedding include:

- Ceremonial props you'll need (such as votive and lighter for a candle ceremony)
- Freshly charged cell phone
- Deodorant or powder
- Cash for bridge tolls and emergencies
- Bottle of water, bag of trail mix
- Music for your road trip

Bring the directions and all your questionnaire notes so you can review them in a quiet moment, especially the names of your witnesses and the family member names and dynamics.

Check your breath out of consideration for the couple, for you will talk with them in close proximity today and on their wedding day. Take a mint. Avoid garlic in your lunch. If you had coffee, brush. Try to do a last-minute face, hands, fingernails, and clothing inspection.

Plan your trip so you can arrive at the rehearsal site at least thirty minutes before you are expected. Will it be hot? Windy? Are you on a lawn? Walk around the site to get a feel for the terrain and an understanding of audio issues. You can expect some members of your wedding party to arrive late because of traffic or misdirection—and some will not show up at all. When everyone arrives, there will be a bit of the hubbub that accompanies family reunions. Try to connect with all the parents as well as members of the wedding party.

chapter five

MANAGING THE REHEARSAL

The point of having a rehearsal is to flush out problems. When you find, address, and clear up issues, you decrease the chance of confusion on the wedding day. Thanks to your rehearsal, members of the wedding party will know where they are supposed to walk and who is standing beside them. The parents will know where to sit. Your bride and groom will not be surprised by the sequence of events, and they will know the correct hand upon which to place their rings. Readers will have had a chance to test their voices.

The rehearsal also acts as a bridge between wedding as concept, which may have lasted a year or more, and the actual wedding. The bride might carry a stand-in wedding bouquet fashioned from ribbons culled from earlier festivities. There is something profound and sobering for the couple about going through the motions, even amidst the joy and mild chaos of the rehearsal. You may also witness this internal process in the parents, especially during the rehearsing of the processional.

A typical rehearsal should take forty minutes or less, though it can go much longer if your wedding party has been drinking beforehand. I'm just saying.

ON ARRIVAL AT THE REHEARSAL SITE

When you see the bride and groom:

Get the license.

Get the license.

Get the license. Then, put the license safely away.

You have arrived at the rehearsal site. You may or may not work with a wedding coordinator. There are two kinds of coordinators. A site facilitator (often called the "day of the wedding" coordinator) will know everything about the facility, will be there on the wedding day, and might already have a personal routine for conducting rehearsals. Or an actual wedding coordinator, who has worked from the beginning with the couple, may be on hand. If either is present and she wishes to conduct the rehearsal of the processional and the recessional, let her. You will still lead the walk-through of your ceremony.

There is also a distinct possibility that *no* coordinator will be on hand. Maybe the bride coordinated the entire wedding herself, or relied on friends and family. Perhaps the wedding is in someone's home, or you are in a place where the site person will do nothing more than show up to open the doors on the wedding day. In the case of no coordinator, *you* become the sole authority for the rehearsal. Follow the tips laid out in this chapter. The skills you gain here will help you go far in any future career as a cat herder.

WHICH SIDE FOR THE BRIDE?

Generally the groom stands to the right of the altar (which is *your* left) and the bride to the left of the altar (*your* right), except it's the reverse in Jewish weddings. The bride-on-the-left tradition stems from the old days of marriage by capture, when the groom had to leave his right hand—which he used to hold his sword—free in the event that he should need to defend his bride from other suitors. On the other hand, Jewish brides stand on the right side of the chuppah (wedding canopy), based on an interpretation of Psalms 45:9: "The queen stands on your right hand in fine gold of Ophir."

The old tradition of seating all of the bride's family on her side and the groom's family and friends on his side is weaker than it has been in the past. Couples often don't care where anyone sits as long as the front row is reserved for key members of the family and perhaps any readers or other guests with a direct involvement in the wedding ceremony rituals.

Reserving that front row is important. Wedding coordinators take care of this, but in absence of one, remind your couple that they might need to create or delegate place cards for those seats. In a casual wedding I attended, guests were told to sit wherever they liked. A family of five sat in the front row on one side, leaving one seat. The bride arrived accompanied by both her parents. When bride met groom, the parents turned to sit and found just one seat open. They stood until one of the young men rose and moved elsewhere, allowing them a second seat. This flustered the parents and embarrassed the young man, and could have been avoided.

HOW TO SEIZE THE REINS

You can expect any number of interesting factors at your rehearsal. One day I stood on a lawn near some natural hot springs, waiting for the bride and groom and making small talk with the coordinators for nearly three hours. There were no chairs. I watched the sun set. The couple had decided to go to a large city to get their wedding license around lunchtime that day, and then they got stuck in Saturday traffic. They arrived just as the elaborate rehearsal dinner began, preempting any time for us. Perhaps your wedding party is quite large or rambunctious, or half of them aren't there at all. Maybe children are running around, there is a language barrier, or the rehearsal location is not the actual wedding location. Don't be disturbed.

When everyone arrives at rehearsal, expect a certain amount of milling around and conversation as family members and friends greet each other, frequently not having seen each other for a long time. Give them ten minutes of this but no longer. They can catch up at the rehearsal dinner or the wedding reception, but now they—and you— have a job to do.

Call for attention, and when they settle and face you expectantly, introduce yourself by your name and your title: "I'm so-and-so, and I will be your officiant for this wedding." Even if everyone there is a close relative of yours, this introduction will alert them that, at least for today and the wedding day, you are playing a specific and important role. It will improve the quality of their attention.

From that point, remember that a great way to get people to follow your instruction is to communicate constantly. Try not to jump around: go step by step, be patient, and speak clearly. When you get to tricky parts, tell your party what you and they are about to do, explain what you are doing while you do it, and then summarize what you did. Here are some examples:

- "Now we are going to go through the motions of the ceremony."
- "Now I'd like each reader to come up, choose two lines at random from your reading, and say them loudly so those in the back can hear. This gives you a chance to test how your voice will carry."
- "OK, we have completed the recessional, and that went smoothly. Anyone have any questions about their part? No? OK, everybody, that's a wrap."

WHY TO REHEARSE STARTING IN THE MIDDLE

A wedding can be seen as three parts. It opens with the *processional*, in which all members of the wedding party arrive at the altar. Next, the *ceremony* transforms the bride and groom into a married couple. Finally, all members of the wedding party leave the altar in the *recessional*.

Many officiants and coordinators like to rehearse the wedding in this order: ceremony first, recessional, and then the processional. Although this sequence might seem counterintuitive, it accomplishes so many good things that I find it to be the most efficient and preferable way to rehearse. Here's how to explain the benefits to your wedding party.

Say, "We will start with the ceremony to give everyone a chance to see where you'll be standing, and who is standing on either side of you. After the ceremony, we will naturally move on toward the recessional. This sequence makes the line-up for the processional easier for everyone. That's why we are going to start with the ceremony, with everyone lined up just as they will be. Bride and groom, let's start with you—follow me to the altar."

CEREMONY: THE LINE-UP

In a traditional church wedding, the bride and groom often face the officiant with their backs to their guests. Because the officiant is on a dais above the couple, that's where guests focus their attention. The contemporary approach focuses attention, instead, on the marrying couple. Typically, they form the center of a semicircle made up of all the members of the wedding party, and they face both each other and their guests. If a wedding is a small one, they may stand within the circle of their guests.

Once you line up every wedding-party member as if the ceremony is about to start, the bridesmaids and groomsmen can look to their right and left to learn who is on either side of them. Position the bride and groom about arm's length in front of you, close enough to each other so they can hold hands but far apart enough so you can speak through them to the crowd. They should stand so they can see each other and you, and so they can turn to their guests if they wish.

The wedding party fans out behind the couple, evenly spaced so each one can be seen, and facing diagonally so they can see both the guests and the bride and groom. You may encounter space issues in your location. Adapt to them. For the best photos, each bridesmaid should hold her bouquet in front of her solar plexus; each groomsman can hold his hands in front of him in what is called the fig leaf. Or the men can stand with their hands behind them, looking a little more military. No one should have crossed arms or hands in their pockets.

Now ask the bride and groom to survey their wedding party and see if they want to make any changes due to height variations or other considerations. It's their wedding vision—there's no right or wrong in this.

Take a moment to encourage the wedding party to relax and keep breathing. You can also mention that they might want to drink water and eat a good breakfast before the big event. Alert the best man that on the wedding day you'll look to him for the rings. Alert the maid of honor that she'll be on point to fluff or smooth the back of the bride's dress, and also to receive and hold the bride's bouquet before any rituals begin, such as candle lighting or the ring exchange.

CEREMONY: MOTIONS AND CUES

Once everyone lines up to satisfaction, and the parents and any other stray guests are seated (or, if no chairs were set out, are off at a distance), you can rehearse the ceremony.

You don't have to read any of your words aloud. Instead, glance at each page of your script and talk about the sections of the wedding to find anything that needs to be addressed and rehearsed. You can say things like, "Now I'll mention the importance of family," or, "We'll have a pause here."

Make sure that you are pronouncing names correctly for the bride, groom, readers, and anyone else you will call up. If you have one or more readings, and if the readers are present, ask each one to come up. Give them their cue (the last phrase you'll say before it's their turn) from your script, and ask them to find a couple of lines from the middle of their reading, stand up straight, and read the lines loudly and slowly to the back of your audience. The readers might find that they must both speak up and slow down. Let them do it a couple of times until they feel comfortable. This step alone often encourages them to go home and rehearse again before the big day. Remind the readers, and the bride and groom, that they can speak a little more slowly than they are tempted to, since our first instinct is to rush right through to the end. They can also pause if they need to. From any audience's point of view, slower speech and pauses indicate emotion and thoughtfulness.

Your bride and groom will not have to speak their vows at rehearsal unless they want to, but you will talk about them. As you have cued the readers, likewise, let your bride and groom know the few words you will say just before their "I do" or recitation of vows is needed. As the vows begin, the bride will want to give her bouquet to the maid of honor (if she hasn't already done so) so she can hold her groom's hands.

Reassure them that if they need to repeat something you're saying, you'll give them just a few words at a time, such as "To have and to hold." They may be worried about flubbing one of the most important moments of their lives. Help alleviate their anxiety by letting them know you are here to support them, not to make anything harder. That's why you have copies on hand of the readings and any vows that they've written—this emotional ceremony is not the time for anyone to have to recite from memory. If they insist on memorizing anyway, let them. And if they bring handwritten vows on the wedding day, that's okay too. Some people just can't write what they want to say until the last minute.

As rituals appear in your script, you will walk through the motions (see ritual details in part two of this book). Make rehearsing the rituals fun, miming them with the couple and any other guests who are involved. Going through the motions will make the movements familiar to them on the wedding day, when their minds are in an "altared" state.

When the time comes to discuss the rings, show the bride and groom that if they grasp each other's left hand as if they are shaking hands, it becomes easy for the groom to find the bride's correct ring finger—and if they keep holding hands but flip them over, there is the correct ring finger for the groom. The bride may have an engagement ring on her left hand already, so remind her to move it to her right hand on the wedding day.

Stress can cause a ring finger to swell up a whole size on the wedding day. If either bride or groom encounters a lot of resistance as they put the ring on each other's finger, tell them not to push it, but to release the other's hand and let him or her push it the rest of the way over the knuckle. No one will notice but them. You might have them practice this.

The couple may have decided to ask for participation from the wedding guests and, of course, most guests are not at the rehearsal. If the couple has asked for blessings from family and friends at ceremony's end, or for a group response, give the wedding party and family cues about what to say and when to say it. Their response will guide the rest of the guests on the wedding day.

At the end of the rehearsal ceremony, you can tell the couple that they can rehearse the kiss. This always brings smiles, and they will probably kiss.

REHEARSING THE RECESSIONAL

After the kiss is the natural point to start recessing. I encourage the bride and groom to remember, at this same point on their wedding day, to stop for a moment, look at their guests, hold hands, take a breath, and let it all sink in. Then, the bride can turn to her maid of honor to retrieve her bouquet. She can take her new husband's arm or join hands, and they will walk back up the aisle.

To mimic the joining of the bridal couple, the maid of honor and the best man come together, usually once the couple has cleared the last row of guests. She takes his arm and together they recess, followed by the next two in line, and so on.

When the entire wedding party has cleared the stage, move forward and gesture to the bride's parents and family (in the first row) that they can rise and depart, and then do the same for the groom's family.

REHEARSING THE PROCESSIONAL

Having just completed the recessional, it's a good bet that your wedding party now has a fair idea of how to line up for the processional. That's why this sequence saves time; people understand what to shoot for.

If you find yourself with a coordinator who prefers to line up the processional first, go with it. Help that person herd the wedding party into place and plan on possibly re-rehearsing the processional if anyone has switched places during the ceremony. Have patience as people mill around and finish their conversations.

A coordinator advises the wedding party where and when to gather just before the ceremony. If there is no coordinator, discuss the gathering location and time with the couple, and then advise the wedding party. The gathering place will often be to one side of the ceremony space about ten minutes before the ceremony begins.

In a typical line-up, you lead, followed by the groom. Sometimes he is accompanied by his parents. The groomsmen usually follow the groom. After a pause and perhaps a change of music, the bridesmaids file in. The bride and groom might decide to have bridesmaids and groomsmen enter together as couples instead of the traditional line of men first, followed by the women.

Once you have arrived at your spot on the altar, watch as the others come in. Give them an encouraging nod or a smile. Be on hand to untangle any confusion.

The bridesmaids are followed by children (if they are part of the wedding party) bearing rings and flowers. The scattering of flower petals signifies a new, never trodden path for the bride to walk down as she approaches her life transformation. When the flower bearers are really young, they forget to scatter petals, but that's all right.

The ring bearer(s) should rehearse walking the rings all the way to the best man, who should be ready to take them. The best man might need to untie the rings from a pillow to put them into his pocket (or on a couple of fingers) for later in the ceremony.

Any children under the age of five who are part of the wedding party should be accompanied, or at least closely watched, by a designated adult. The same is true for pets, as dogs are occasionally called upon to bear the rings. A word to the wise: let parents guide their children.

After ring and flower bearers, there may be another pause, another change of music. When the bride approaches, often accompanied by one or both parents, say to the guests something like, "Will all rise to greet the bride?" At the rehearsal, you may need to say it twice, as your few guests are still chatting in their seats.

As bridesmaids and any children arrive, advise your groom to get ready for an important movement that is called, in the wedding trade, the hand-off. The bride should approach close to the altar but not all the way, and stop. If she is accompanied, this becomes her opportunity to say her farewell to those who accompanied her. Once

THE OFFICIANT'S PRESENCE AT THE REHEARSAL IS SO IMPORTANT

Stacy McCain,
Stacy McCain Event Planners, SAN FRANCISCO, CALIFORNIA

You have worked with the couple all along. When you come to the rehearsal, it's a continuation of the relationship you've built, and it calms them to know that you were here today, and you'll be there tomorrow.

I can wrangle (coordinate) a rehearsal if I have to, but when the new officiant arrives the next day, it's hard to find that very small window of time, during a hectic day, to give the officiant his or her cues. If you arrive at three-thirty and the ceremony is at four, I might be pinning boutonnieres, checking in with catering, helping the musicians, or getting something for the bride. The wedding goes vastly better when the officiant knows what to do already.

she does that, encourage the groom to step forward and make his gesture of respect or affection to the parent(s) or other(s) accompanying the bride. That might look like a handshake or a hug, if they are close. Then, the bride's escort(s) should take their seat(s), and the groom can lead his bride up to you.

If the bride is unaccompanied, she can still stop, and the groom can step forward to escort her to the altar. In rehearsal, once the bride and groom are in front of you, let them know that they have completed the processional. Ask them if they are comfortable with it, or if they would like to go through it again. Either way, since your entire wedding party is up there, go ahead and recess just as you have practiced. If you did the processional first, just rehearse the ceremony, then recess.

Once the couple has signed off on everything, announce to all the guests that rehearsal has been successful, it is over, and they can move on to their next event. Check in one last time with the couple and remind them to delegate any last-minute tasks. A bride shouldn't feel forced to spend the evening before her wedding reviewing the seating chart, or the last few minutes before her ceremony building floral centerpieces.

I cannot promise that everything will go smoothly on the wedding day. But because you just rehearsed, you have reduced your risk of chaos by about 95 percent.

A NEW OFFICIANT SPEAKS

I WISH WE'D REHEARSED

Adela Basayne, PORTLAND, OREGON

My friend turned to me and said, "You do weddings, don't you?" And I said, "Sure." The bride was looking for something Jewish. I knew a lot about Jewish weddings, including my own. I went online to ULC and ordained myself. Anita Diamant's *A New Jewish Wedding* was a great resource. We exchanged drafts, added in a wine ceremony, and took out a sonnet. I rehearsed my own part since I had not actually written those words; I had to get a feel for those rhythms.

I wish the couple had been able to rehearse with me beforehand. It would have helped to choreograph their wedding friends who held the posts of the chuppah. But the couple really wanted things to flow spontaneously, so I honored that wish. Overall, the wedding was lovely, successful, and very sincere, but the chuppah did turn out to be a little too short for the couple, and they poured too much wine into their glasses, so they had to chug it to finish!

chapter six

THE WEDDING DAY

We stood on the marble patio of a bazillion-dollar mansion that overlooked Pebble Beach. Behind me, emerald-velvet lawns disappeared into the dark-blue calm of the Pacific. The late October sun shone gently. The bride had just appeared at the French doorway arm in arm with her father. That's when a golf ball whizzed past my ear and ricocheted off the house.

A wedding can be a joyful, profound, magical occasion. It draws families and friends together in celebration, and people are nearly always happy to attend. There is also a wild card at every wedding, and you don't know where it will pop up, because these multipart ceremonies include so many moving variables: timing, props, cues, rituals, members of the wedding party, guests, vendors, passersby—in short: people, and all of their quirks.

You might have rehearsed a ceremony to perfection, but there's no way to account for every variable on the big day. Every wedding has a life of its own. People arrive from far-flung places in different states of mind. A florist arrives late; a bridesmaid is stung by a wasp; a shuttle hasn't arrived; someone just insulted the groom's mother. Weather, children's tummies, feuding parents, stray allergies—you won't know where your wild card will come from, but trust that there will be one.

Rather than let a little mishap run amok and blindside you, stay aware of your surroundings and keep calm. Prepare as much as you can with the wedding-day checklist that begins on the facing page, and then enjoy the ride.

DID YOU SKIP THE REHEARSAL?

Some people skip the rehearsal because the wedding party is small, or the ritual will be simple. If this is true for the wedding you are about to perform, I encourage you to go back and read the rehearsal chapter anyway. You'll find important items there, such as why people stand in certain places, how the wedding ring is most easily slipped on, and what you can do to support your bride and groom. You'll know what to expect before it actually happens, and you'll be able to run the ceremony as smoothly as possible.

FILL OUT THE LICENSE

On the morning of the wedding, if you have not already done this, review the marriage license and whatever came with it. There might be an envelope in which to mail the license, or you'll need to provide your own. The address of where to mail the license is usually somewhere on the license.

Now look at the license and carefully fill in your part. Take the time to print legibly. Some licenses specify that you use black ink to fill them out, other licenses ask for black, blue, or dark ink. I always have two black-ink pens just to play it safe.

Make sure to write the date of the wedding using numbers instead of words: For example, write 08/25/2015 rather than August 25.

Never write out the month. If you have been ordained, you can write "nondenom." on the line reserved for denomination, and "minister" on the line for your role. If you have been deputized, put a long dash on the denomination line, and write "deputy" as your role.

Double check the correct county in which you will marry the couple. A wedding license was once returned to me because I had written the neighboring county by mistake. It's easy to check: Identify the town or city in which the couple is marrying. Then go online to a search engine such as Google or Bing. Type in your town/city and state, and add the word "county." Some couples will marry in an unincorporated territory, in which case, choose the closest town and be sure to list that town as the marriage location.

Leave the spaces for witness signatures and your signature blank. You will add those after the wedding. Do not cross out, add to, cover up, or alter any part of the license in any way, because the county recorder's office will reject any certificate that has been altered.

You may be given a souvenir marriage certificate, which you can also fill out and bring to the wedding along with the legal license. It might be accompanied by a booklet about having children or other marriage issues. Dispose of this unless you think it is new and must-have information for the couple. Now you are ready to get to the wedding.

WEDDING-DAY CHECKLIST

The points that follow, which were hard-won over scores of weddings, will save you time and worry. Make sure you have:

- The script for your ceremony in a thin binder or bound however you choose.
- Any readings, printed separately in a larger font, and bound so they can easily be read.
- Your interview notes so you can review everything, especially unfamiliar names.

- The license. If you have it, bring it. If you do not, make it your first order of business on arrival at the wedding to acquire the license and fill in your part.

- Directions to the ceremony venue and to the reception venue if they are different.

- Two black pens to fill out the license. Bring two in case one leaks or dries up. Slip these and the interview notes into the back pocket of your binder.

- Breath mints. Pop two of these as you wait for the processional to begin as a courtesy to your wedding couple. Try not to eat garlic or onions that day. Brush your teeth after you drink coffee.

- A clean handkerchief for the bride or groom. One or the other may start to weep at an important juncture, and your small gesture of offering a clean hanky will do worlds of good. When that happens, take your time to let them adjust and settle again before you go on with the ceremony. The guests will not be impatient—this is the stuff of weddings, so they will be agreeably moved. The groom is just as likely to tear up as the bride. Clean handkerchiefs have also come to the rescue when a bee was attracted to the bride's flowers, and in one wine-country summer wedding where the sunshine was so hot, the bride's foundation started to trickle down her chin. In all my weddings, I have received just two cleaned-and-returned hankies. So tuck one into your pocket or your binder and prepare to never see it again.

- A watch. Your cell phone will be off during the wedding, right? But somehow you can count on being asked what time it is before the ceremony, especially by nervous groomsmen.

- Extra deodorant, lip balm, sunscreen, stockings if appropriate, and a comb.

- Any props for your wedding. For lighting a candle, bring a votive and a lighter or book of matches. If the couple is handfasting, bring the length of ribbon. You might need a pocket knife or manicure scissors in case the wedding rings are tied too tightly to their pillow.

- A snack and a bottle of water.

Check that your outfit is clean and neat, and your shoes are appropriate to the landscape. Ladies, lawns tend to suck up stiletto heels.

With all parts assembled, leave early enough so you can arrive at least an hour early, and tune in to your local news station to check traffic conditions. Bon voyage!

A NEW OFFICIANT SPEAKS

PREPARING MY TABLET FOR THE WEDDING

Chris Reimer, ST. LOUIS, MISSOURI

I saved the completed wedding script as a PDF. That's because you can take a PDF file anywhere, even when the Internet connection isn't there. I saved the PDF as an iBook in my iPad, making the font about eighteen points so I wouldn't have to squint to read it. I tried to break the ceremony into spots where there would be a natural pause. It took up eight page screens. On the wedding day, I checked my iPad about ten times to make sure it was properly charged. I also had a back-up script on paper in a nice leather folder.

PREPARE YOUR PUBLIC-SPEAKING VOICE

When you perform the wedding, you'll speak both *to* the couple and *past* them. To do this, you'll direct your voice to the back of the audience and project it loudly enough without shouting. You also want people in the back to understand the words you are saying. You can warm up your voice, and also flex your face muscles, by singing in the car along the way. Use a song that makes you feel good, one that contains both low and high notes. Sing softly, then loudly. Stick out your tongue. Blow through your lips wetly and rudely, like a four-year-old. Extra points for making yourself laugh. Actors and singers use these exercises to warm up.

Finally, try this five-minute exercise to sharpen your diction. It is said to exercise every single muscle in your mouth. First, recite the following nursery rhyme:

> *Mary had a little lamb; its fleece was white as snow.*
> *And everywhere that Mary went, the lamb was sure to go.*

Next, stick out your tongue and hold on to the end of it, and slowly recite the same verse. It will sound like this: "Mawy hathe a lithel lamm." Don't let go of your tongue, and pronounce every sound as completely as you can. Now let go of your tongue and recite the verse one last time. Listen to your suddenly crisp *d*s and *t*s.

SETTLING IN AT THE WEDDING

I chatted with a groomsman from Seattle just before one wedding ceremony began. "We had a friend officiate at our wedding," he remarked.

"How did it go?"

"She cried through the whole ceremony."

A weeping officiant might touch hearts for a moment, but after that it gets awkward or, worse, irritating. Attention and sympathy should flow to the couple, not to you. Fortunately, you have a useful tool that will center you and remind you of why you are here and what you came to accomplish. I call it your *Power Hour*.

The key to your Power Hour is to arrive an hour before the ceremony is scheduled to begin. Here is what you'll do with those sixty minutes.

CHECK IN

In the first fifteen minutes, find your couple or the wedding coordinator to let them know that you are here. This gives them an immediate sense of relief—they can check your arrival off their lists. Next, scout out your altar, and check to see that all the props you need are available and ready. If something is missing, you'll have a little time to either get it fixed or work your way around it.

COME TO YOUR SENSES

Now that you have made your presence known, it's time to get out of the way of the mad rush that precedes a wedding. You're likely to see the photographer snapping photos of the wedding party, florists putting final changes on the altar, and caterers setting up lemonade for the first guests. The bride is still probably having her makeup done. This is your chance to ground yourself and find your center, or, if you don't speak Californian, to calm your nerves and tap into something deeper.

Turn off your phone. If this is an outdoor wedding, you may be able to walk a little bit. Consciously relax. If you are at all anxious, try to locate that pocket of anxiety in your body, and breathe it out. Methodically check in with each of your five senses to bring your mind fully into the present moment.

COMPOSE YOURSELF

It's the third quarter of your Power Hour. Now that you have reached a still point, despite everyone rushing around you, it's time to glance through your script, put on your robe or stole or special outfit, and check your breath. If you didn't already do voice and diction exercises on the ride over, do something now. It's time for your last bathroom break, last washing of hands. Check your clothes and your teeth in a mirror if possible.

CONNECT AND SUPPORT

You have prepared yourself; now, in the final quarter, go out and connect with people. Find the best man and, if any, the ring bearers: Who has the rings? Find the musicians and consult with them: Will you or the coordinator cue them to start the processional music? Tell them your last line in the script (usually "You may kiss the bride") so they know when to start the recessional music. It is likewise good manners to let the photographer know about any special ritual in the ceremony, and ask him or her if there is any particular photography request. The photographer will appreciate it if you can remember to step aside during intimate bride-and-groom moments, so she or he can capture the best portrait. Do what you can, but remember to relax if it is not perfect.

If there is a DJ or videographer, he or she will probably want to attach a small microphone to your collar or notebook. Line up with your groom and his men, and let your relaxed good humor calm them down.

Weddings rarely start on time. No matter how long it takes, it's not your problem. On a rare occasion, you may be called on to calm a bride's nerves. When that happens, encourage her to talk and listen carefully and respectfully. When people feel truly heard, they tend to arrive at their own solutions.

A COORDINATOR CAUTIONS

ARRIVE ON TIME OR EARLY

Tina Reikes

OWNER AND COORDINATOR OF

Bear Flag Farms, WINTERS, CALIFORNIA

It's so important for the officiant to arrive by his or her scheduled time, usually forty-five minutes before the ceremony or earlier. When you arrive early, both the couple and the coordinator can relax a little more. When you are late, however, you suddenly become a problem, and the level of anxiety for bride, groom, and coordinator grows every minute you are not there.

Most professional planners have lists of cell numbers for each vendor and staff member, including the officiant. Please contact the coordinator the moment you realize there might be a delay. That lets the coordinator quickly start to resolve any potential problem that might affect the wedding ceremony, and find a suitable replacement for you if necessary.

Author's note: Put the coordinator's phone number, the groom's number, and the number of your personal back-up in your phone.

THREE . . . TWO . . . ONE . . . YOU'RE ON!

As you line up with the groomsmen, take a moment to focus on the groom, who is likely to be nervous. You can reassure him: Let him know that he looks good, shake his hand, and say something like, "Welcome to the next chapter of your life." Confirm that the best man has the rings, or that the ring bearer knows what to do with them.

YOUR ENTRANCE

As you walk in, either along the side of the gathering or leading the processional down the aisle, look at the crowd and stay in the moment. Arrive at your mark (the place where you stood at rehearsal) and make sure the groom hits his mark. Stand tall and centered. Smile or remain solemn, but don't force anything. This is not the time to wipe your nose or tug at your clothing. It's not about you.

LOOK TO THE BRIDE

After you, the groom, and his men arrive, escorts will seat parents, and then the bridesmaids arrive, followed by the ring- and flower-bearing children. At that point, there is a moment of silence before the music changes to signal the coming of the bride. From your vantage point, you can see the bride approach first. The groom is probably also looking for her, and the guests are partly looking at his reaction and partly twisting around to see the bride. When you see her, call out clearly, "Will all rise, please, for the bride?"

She will enter slowly or quickly, escorted or unescorted. If she's accompanied, here again is the sequence of motions referred to as the hand-off: Bride and escort (often the father) stop, bride bids farewell to escort if she wishes, groom approaches with (optional) gesture of respect or affection to the escort, escort falls back, and groom leads bride to altar. If she is unaccompanied, when she approaches the altar encourage your groom to step forward and help her up to her spot in front of you. Take a moment to welcome her, and to let her settle; her maid of honor will fix her veil and train. She can hand her bouquet to the maid of honor now or later.

A WEDDING PLANNER'S PERSPECTIVE

TIPS FOR NEW OFFICIANTS

Alison Hotchkiss,

OWNER OF

Alison Events Planning and Design, SAN FRANCISCO, CALIFORNIA

AUTHOR OF

All the Essentials Wedding Planner:
The Ultimate Tool for Organizing Your Big Day

I've worked with both professional and amateur officiants, and had a chance to really observe them in action. Here are my biggest take-aways over the years for any new officiant:

- Remind people to stand for the bride, and remind them to sit down.

- Check your voice for volume and pitch. Rehearse so you can project your voice loudly enough to the back row. I'm not a huge fan of microphones because they interrupt the visual aesthetic, they pick up any wind that is blowing, and they increase the risk of faulty technology spoiling the ceremony. So try to do without a microphone if the wedding is fewer than seventy-five people.

- Keep your outdoor ceremony short and sweet, especially if it is hot or you are on a beach. For beach weddings, do it at low tide. If there are surfers, forget it—your audience will watch the surfers instead of the couple. They can't help it.

- Think about your environment. If the weather changes or your bride is freezing or boiling with no shade, shorten your script. Adjust to acts of nature: a dog barking, a child screaming, a helicopter. Stop, let the noise pass, and then continue. Make light of it, be witty.

- If it starts to rain, remind the couple that in several cultures, rain is very good luck indeed. It is a sign of fertility!

—— BEGIN YOUR SCRIPT ——

One common mistake that new officiants make is racing through their scripts. Say, "You may be seated." Take this moment, as the guests seat themselves, to breathe and relax.

Speak slowly and clearly. You will be speaking both *to* the couple and *past* the couple to the guests at different times. Change your voice, and look at the bride and groom when you mention their names. When you speak to the guests, aim your voice between the heads of the couple and give it power from your diaphragm. Step to the side during rituals so that the couple takes center stage.

During the ceremony, you will facilitate and manage elements such as:

- **THE FORMAL PAUSE.** To time a pause properly, you can count slowly to twelve or say a silent prayer.

- **AN INFORMAL PAUSE.** Be aware of the couple's needs; pause long enough to allow tears, laughter, adjustments, baby cries, planes passing overhead.

- **EACH RITUAL YOU HAVE CHOSEN.** The guests are watching your motions, so don't speed through them. If you perform a wine ceremony, take your time with the glasses. Make sure each person is actually holding the glass before you let go. Encourage them to slow down. No one wants red wine on a wedding dress. If the couple lights a candle, do your best to make sure it doesn't blow out (or plan to relight it). If you tie a handfasting ribbon, make sure it is secure.

- **THE VOWS AND/OR NOTES OF APPRECIATION.** Pull them from your binder and hand them upright to the person about to read them. If you are saying phrases for them to repeat, keep each phrase short and clear.

- **THE RING EXCHANGE.** Hold the rings in your palm and hand the groom the bride's ring first.

- **THE KISS.** As you tell them they can kiss, take a step back and to the side so that you are out of the way—so that the couple is all anyone sees.

After the bride and groom kiss, and acknowledge their guests, the bride can retrieve her bouquet, then take the groom's arm and together they can head back up the aisle. You can motion to the wedding party to come together and recess up the aisle after them. Then motion to the first-row families that they can rise and follow. Traditionally, the bride's family rises first.

GIVE THE GUESTS GUIDANCE

Before or after you usher that first row, you can make a brief announcement to the guests if the couple has requested it. Some couples prefer to be alone for a few minutes, or they may have agreed to gather with family and the wedding party for photographs. Whatever they decide, it will be generous of you to advise the guests what will happen next and where they can find refreshments. You can be formal or informal:

- "Megan and Devin wish to spend the first few moments of their marriage alone together. Please follow the wedding party to the patio for refreshments, and the couple will rejoin you shortly (or, meet you again at the reception)."
- "Hi, folks, we've been asked to keep the families here for photographs, and the rest of you can proceed to the cocktail hour by the swimming pool."

Your next move is to gather yourself and your binder and walk back up the aisle. Be open to anyone who approaches you, but right now, liquid refreshment is probably uppermost on most of their minds. As for you, your job now is to get your witnesses.

chapter seven

AFTER THE CEREMONY

The first wedding I ever officiated at was for my stepbrother and his bride. They bought me an airplane ticket, and I flew across the country. On the morning of the wedding day, my husband, Mark; my ten-year-old daughter, Peggy; and I drove from Connecticut to an estate in New Jersey. My mother and many family members, including a beloved great-uncle who had performed weddings as a Navy chaplain, sat in the audience. My palms were wet all morning, and I went over and over the ceremony during the drive. I had my robe, my breath mints, and the black binder holding the wedding ceremony. The binder's back pocket held the license and a black pen for the witnesses' signatures.

The ceremony took place in a beautiful sunken garden. Once I stood in my spot at the top of some wide old steps, all but the wedding couple receded into the background, and we settled into a natural pace. They exchanged vows and rings and transformed into a married couple. The DJ in a nearby tent started some party music, and I changed out of my robe, put everything in the car, and ran to join my family.

We ate, laughed, drank, and ate some more. Many people came up and congratulated me on the performance—even my great-uncle. After the sun set, everyone danced. Late into the night, Mark and I said our good-byes, carried our tired child to the car, and drove away. We had crossed the state line and were deep into Connecticut when Mark casually asked, "So, was it hard to get the witnesses to sign the license?"

The *witnesses!*

I had completely forgotten to get the signatures. The license had sat, unremembered, in the back pocket of the black binder in the trunk of our car. We screeched around and tore back to the wedding site. It took another couple of hours to get back. By this time, the tent had been largely dismantled, the guests long gone—except for my step-sister, who had just come back for a forgotten jacket. She and her husband were the only people left on the premises who had actually seen the wedding. My hands shook as I handed the wedding license to them. Their signatures made the wedding legal.

Don't let this happen to you. Get your signatures immediately after the ceremony, before the champagne, and put your legal documents away before the festivities begin. The following tips will help you negotiate this administrative part of the wedding.

WITNESSING THE LICENSE

After the wedding party leaves the altar and the guests disperse a little, find your two witnesses. They may be milling around with champagne, or standing with the wedding party for photographs. Steer them to a place where they can sign the license. Tell them that this is a legal document and there can be no cross-outs, so they should take their time to sign, print their names, and write their street addresses all the way to the zip code.

Here are some other things to keep in mind:

- The bride and groom already signed the license when they purchased it.
- You and the witnesses must sign the license in dark, durable ink.
- If you haven't already done so, follow the instructions in "Fill Out the License" in chapter six, page 80.
- Keep pen marks inside the lines of the boxes. Tell your witnesses to curb their flourishes so their signatures are inside the boxes. Sometimes they go over, and those licenses are usually accepted by the county, but one officiant had to re-do a license for a clerk, based on an overly large signature.
- There may be no changes, alterations, strikeovers, or whiteouts on the marriage license. If a witness does make an error, don't attempt to correct it. Instead, take it to the county clerk in person, and they will recommend the best way to fix it.
- If your county issued a souvenir certificate along with the legal license, your witnesses can sign the souvenir at the same time. You could leave a copy of their wedding script and souvenir certificate as a gift.
- Finally, put the completed marriage license carefully away before enjoying the festivities.

AFTER THE WITNESSING

You have just shown yourself as a person of some solemnity, authority, and grace during the ceremony. Have some champagne, though you might not want to overdo it. You may receive compliments from the guests. Listen deeply, enjoy the moment, and stay modest. If you can point out to the guest that the bride and groom had a hand in the ceremony, do so. When you meet up again with the couple, congratulate them.

FOLLOW UP: MONDAY MORNING'S HOT POTATO

You have arrived at the final steps in your role as officiant. On Monday morning, or on the first legal business day after the wedding, photocopy the license, address the envelope properly, and mail or hand-deliver the original license. Get it done as thoroughly as you can, check everything twice, and do it before you do anything else that might be even remotely distracting.

Make sure to keep that photocopy of the completed license. It can save a lot of trouble if any issues arise. I frequently send the couple another photocopy, telling them it is their *unofficial copy*, and they can apply for their certified copy from the county clerk in about six weeks.

CONGRATULATIONS, YOU'VE DONE IT!

You showed up for your couple. You used the power vested in you to create both a community-witnessed bond and some inspired theater. You got your witnesses, made a copy of the completed license, and filed it. Take a little time to reflect and feel proud of your contribution.

Did you enjoy it, and now feel enormously relieved to never do it again? That's great. Just remember the highs and lows of the whole process and chalk it up as a great education. If you received any compliments, savor them. Get every morsel of enjoyment you can out of this good skill-stretching experience.

If, on the other hand, you loved every part of the process and you'd do it again tomorrow, I'm here to let you know that you can do it again. And again. There are always occasions and life events that need celebrating, and the world needs more good officiants. If you want to conduct weddings as a profession, visit my website to find a free checklist of things to consider as you hang up your shingle: www.lisafrancesca.com.

A NEW OFFICIANT SPEAKS

THEY WANTED THE SERENITY PRAYER, AND THEY WANTED TO HAVE FUN

Art Boudreault, SAN RAFAEL, CALIFORNIA

I interviewed the couple three times. They wanted a brief ceremony, they wanted to use the Serenity Prayer, and they wanted to have fun.

We did a full rehearsal—that is, everything except the vows. Reading aloud helped the readers and the couple to manage any stage fright.

I opened the wedding by describing the Serenity Prayer, and how it related to the steps they were about to take. If you don't already know it, the short form is excellent advice for a marriage, or indeed any venture:

> *God, Grant me the serenity to accept the things*
> *I cannot change,*
> *The courage to change the things I can,*
> *And the wisdom to know the difference.*

The wedding went smoothly. People commented that it had been appropriate, warm, and spiritual. Before I mailed the license, I made color copies, gave one to the couple, and kept the other. It's an additional reminder to them that if they want a certified copy of the license, they'll need to apply for it about six weeks after the wedding.

To a first-timer, I'd say recognize that the officiant is not the principal party—that's the wedding couple. Everything you do or say should be subordinate to that. Also, relax and enjoy the humor.

part two

WEDDING RITUALS, READINGS, AND RESOURCES

*I*n this part of the book, you will find rituals (chapter eight) and readings (chapter nine) categorized by subject or culture. Chapter ten lists useful printed and online wedding-ceremony resources.

chapter eight

WEDDING-CEREMONY RITUALS

Here are examples of what you might say and do as you perform one ritual or another that is appropriate to the couple and to their wedding. You can easily tailor the sections and add them to your draft of the ceremony once you have an outline in place (see chapter three for how to do that).

People have different tastes in material. Some passages that follow might strike you as overly sentimental, or some lighter pieces may not seem appropriately serious while others appear too serious. Use only what feels natural to you and the couple, and feel free to revise or abandon anything that doesn't.

RITUALS THAT SIGNIFY THE UNION

A ritual involves gestures, sometimes words, and sometimes objects, in order to physically signify the transformation that is taking place.

The following rituals are about bonding, either between the community and the couple, or family and the couple, or between the marrying couple themselves.

BLESSING OF THE RINGS BY THE COMMUNITY

YOU: Friends, today some of you will participate in an unusual and personal ritual. Monique and Cody have asked you to bless their rings. John, as best man, is holding both rings. Now he will pass these rings among the families and the wedding party. Please take them carefully and bless them silently. When we are ready for the rings, I'll ask you to hand them up to me.

After the vows: May I have the rings please? *To the community:* You have blessed, with your love, the giving of these rings.

Monique and Cody, let us witness the sealing of your promises with these rings.

CANDLE LIGHTING

In this example, the mothers light the candle. However, anyone dear to the couple can light them. If the bride and/or groom have older children, the children may light the candles.

YOU: It has been written that from every human being there rises a light that reaches straight to heaven. And when two souls who are destined for each other find one another, their streams of light flow together, and a single brighter light goes forth from their united being. Donna and Charlotte, as the mothers of this couple, Jeff and Angelique are grateful to you for your love, guidance, and support. They would now like you to light the candles they will use as they formally commit themselves to one another. *Donna and Charlotte each light a candle and hand them to their children. Then together, Jeff and Angelique light a larger candle.*

— HONORING CHILDREN —

YOU: Jonathan and Eleanor, the two of you are combining your strengths and hopes in this marriage. However, this marriage will affect more than just the two of you. Your decision to marry also affects the lives of Alex and Gregory. Today we acknowledge the creation of a marriage and the enhancement of a family. Will you both promise to give Gregory and Alex your understanding, your support, your laughter, your patience, and your warmth, being faithful and loving parents to them both? If so, please answer, "We will."

COUPLE: We will.

Here's another:

YOU: Julianna and James, your decision to marry also deeply affects the life of Hannah Mae. Just as you are committing yourselves to each other, you are also committing yourselves to your child. Today, you declare your solidarity as a family. From today forward, Hannah will have James as another loving adult to help guide and support her.

JAMES: Hannah, thank you for the joy and love you have already given me. I will always be here for you. *James gives a gift to Hannah.*

— SAND CEREMONY —

YOU: Katie and Greg will now perform a ritual to express the joining and intermixing of their lives. They have brought sand from the California coast and from a beach community in New York where Greg and his family have spent considerable time. Once the sands from each vessel are combined, it will be impossible to separate them. *Each pours sand from his or her own vase into a third. This ritual represents the blending of families as well.*

─── WINE CEREMONY ───

This ceremony requires two glasses, partially filled with wine, and a third empty glass. They can rest on a table near you and the couple. It's fine to pour the wine from a bottle at the time of the ritual; it's easier on you if the bottle has already been opened prior to the ceremony.

YOU: Wine is a gift from our earth, the rain, and the sun. From the most ancient of times, drinking from the same cup has been a powerful symbol of agreement, of affection, of peace. Sipping from the same cup is symbolic of the life the couple will share, each giving to the other generously and freely, each receiving from the other fully.

In a variation of this tradition, Gabe and Emma first sip from their own glasses, indicating that they are maintaining their independence and individuality. *They silently toast each other, and then each sips from his or her own glass.*

Then, as a demonstration of the strong bond that exists between them, they exchange glasses and drink. *The couple does this.*

Finally, to symbolize this moment, the beginning of their marriage, each pours some of his or her wine into a third glass, then holds the common glass for the other to drink from. *You hold the third glass steady as they pour their wine into it, and you return their glasses to the table near you. You can plan to put the binder down on the table so your hands are free. The groom gently tips the glass for the bride as she drinks and she does the same for him. When you retrieve the glass from them, place it back on the table or, if you are outside and it feels appropriate, return the dregs of the wine from the shared glass to the earth from which it came.*

A NEW OFFICIANT SPEAKS

SHE ASKED FOR A MAGIC TRICK

Ben Seidman,

RESIDENT MAGICIAN AT

Mandalay Bay Resort & Casino,

LAS VEGAS, NEVADA

Two old friends asked me to officiate at their wedding. I went online to ordain myself and research sample weddings.

I was surprised when Tera, the bride, asked me to perform a magic trick while officiating. I loved the idea of using my magic but also did not want to focus on myself too much; the day was all about them, after all.

Only the couple knew I was the officiant. As they proceeded to the altar, which was outdoors in the Cascades, a guitarist and flutist played music and I accompanied them on a xylophone. When Mike and Tera stopped at the altar, I put down my mallets and joined them, to the great surprise of our mutual friends.

When it came time for the trick, Mike wrote his name on one card and Tera wrote hers on another. After a shuffle, the two cards found each other in the deck, just like when the couple first met. I put both cards in their hands and they magically melted together into one card.

To the new officiant, I'd say take time to write and edit your script. Even though I am a professional performer, I found this to be stressful because it was unlike anything I'd ever done. Spend enough time with your words so you are less affected by nerves on the big day. There's an old stage saying: "Comfort is knowing your lines."

OTHER RITUALS

There are many, many ways to express a couple's togetherness and new life ahead, so follow where the couple's hearts prompt them. One bride and groom requested a patch of cloth sent ahead from each of their guests. From the cloth, they stitched a wedding quilt that the officiant wrapped around them during the ceremony. Another couple planted a small tree, which they committed to nourishing just as they would tend to their new marriage.

In a wedding between two theater people, the bride and groom sang their vows to one another. And at a picnic wedding, the bride and groom shared fresh loaves of bread with their guests as the first meal of their new life together.

CULTURAL AND RELIGIOUS ELEMENTS

These wedding rituals are in alphabetical order, note that some cultures share the same rituals. You can check the Resources section in chapter ten for more ideas. A reminder: if you are deputized rather than ordained, you may not use any religious elements in your wedding.

COINS, CORD OR LASSO, AND VEIL
(from Spain, Mexico, the Philippines)

In these rituals, sponsors, who might be godparents or already married couples, assist you and the couple. A coin bearer carries thirteen coins.

YOU: Zachary, will you bring up the coins, please? These coins are a symbol of prosperity. May the two of you find prosperity in all of its forms in your life together. *Zachary gives you the coins.*

YOU: Marie, Lee, you have committed yourselves to one another, and in so doing, you have also accepted the responsibilities of supporting your family. These coins are a symbol of your support for each other, and your commitment to take care of one another and your family. *You hand the bag or box of coins to Lee.*

LEE: Marie, I give you these coins as a symbol of my love and support for you and our family. *Lee pours the coins into Marie's hands.*

MARIE: Lee, I accept these coins as a symbol of your love and support. Take these coins as a symbol of my love and support for you and our family. *Marie pours the coins back into Lee's hands. He puts them back into the bag or box.*

YOU: I now ask Ben, Anna, and Pacita to come forward to assist in the placing of the veil and the tying of the cord. The veil is a physical manifestation of the vows made by Marie and Lee to love, honor, and cherish one another for all time. The veil clothes them, as do their vows. *Veil sponsors drape and pin the veil of long white tulle on the groom's shoulder and over the bride's head, symbolizing the union of two people clothed as one.*

The cord or lasso symbolizes the tie between Lee and Marie. Its symbolism denotes how all things have a beginning and an end, but when tied it also shows that this bond is never-ending. *Cord sponsors stand up with the cord (a silken rope, a string of flowers, or links of coins) in the form of a figure eight, and loosely place each loop around the shoulders of the couple, symbolizing the infinite bond of marriage. At the end of the ceremony, the sponsors remove the cord and then the veil.*

——— CHRISTIAN WEDDING ELEMENTS ———

Your goal is to keep God or Christ, depending on what the couple wishes, at the center of the wedding as the couple's third party. You can accomplish this by opening and closing the ceremony with blessings, and bringing in prayer. The Lord's Prayer is a favorite.

Consecrating

YOU: The grace and peace of our Lord Jesus Christ be with you. *(Sign of the cross)* We are gathered here today in the presence of God to join this man, Richard, and this woman, Barbara, in holy marriage. We pray for their well-being and happiness.

Another opening:

YOU: Friends, we are gathered here today to witness the marriage of Molly and Greg. Let us acknowledge God's presence here and now, as we celebrate this union of two into one. In the name of the Father, the Son, and of the Holy Spirit.

ALL: Amen.

Prayer

YOU: Jay and Vanessa, in joining your lives may God grant you both love to afford each other a special quality of time together; joy in the accomplishments of one another; understanding that your interests and desires will not always be the same; friendship based on mutual trust; courage to speak of a misunderstanding and to work on a solution before the sun sets; compassion to comfort each other in pain; mirth from each of your senses of humor; and awareness to live each day knowing there is no promise of tomorrow. May God bless you and keep you in the palm of His hand. Amen.

Ring Blessing

YOU: May the peace of Christ live always in your hearts and in your home. The wedding ring becomes the enduring symbol of the promises we have just heard. May I have the rings please? *(Pause)* Bless, O Lord, the giving of these rings that they who wear them may abide in peace and love. Amen.

Pronouncement and Blessing

YOU: I call on all of you to witness that Martha and Michael have exchanged their vows, in the presence of God and this gathering, and according to the laws of the State of California, they are now husband and wife.

May the Lord bless and keep you. May the Lord make his face to shine upon you, and be gracious to you. May the Lord lift up his countenance upon you and give you peace. *(In a wedding in which one or both of the couple have been raised in the Catholic faith, they may ask you to make the sign of the cross and say:* In the name of the Father, and of the Son, and of the Holy Spirit, Amen.)

HANDFASTING
(from African, European, and Celtic Traditions)

YOU: In acknowledgement of their shared ancestry, while Michael and Readie make their pledges to each other, I will bind their hands together in an ancient ritual, signifying the strength and seriousness of their commitment to each other. *Tie the ribbon around their wrists. The ribbon should be long enough to tie a figure eight (you can braid ribbons together, too). Tie the knot loose enough so you can untie it easily. (It might be best for YOU to provide the ribbon. Once a couple gave me ribbon that was short and slippery. I tied and retied the knot, but it kept slipping off, which can too easily be interpreted as bad luck.)*

Your bride and groom can say in turn:

Handfasting for a year and a day,
Bound together for a lifetime.
I will always hold your hand fast
And we shall have the time of our lives.

They can also speak their vows to each other at this time if they choose. Then untie the knot.

HAWAIIAN LEI EXCHANGE

A flower lei consists of about fifty fresh flowers strung on a colorful ribbon and is one of the oldest symbols of Hawaiian culture. The bride and groom give and receive fresh-flower leis as a sign of *aloha*, love, acceptance, and welcome toward each other, similar to a ring exchange. They may also exchange leis with their guests.

> **A Hawaiian marriage prayer:** Now two are becoming one, the black night is scattered, the eastern sky grows bright. At last the great day has come!

INDIAN WEDDING ELEMENTS
(Adapted from Hindu Rituals)

Circling the Sacred Fire

The bride and groom walk around the sacred fire seven times. The bride, representing divine energy, leads the groom in the first three rounds, while the groom leads in the last four rounds, to signify balance and completeness.

The Seven Sacred Steps

The couple takes seven steps together, making a vow with each step:

1. Together we will live with respect for one another.
2. Together we will develop mental, physical, and spiritual balance.
3. Together we will prosper, acquire wealth, and share our accomplishments.
4. Together we will acquire happiness, harmony, and knowledge through mutual love.

5. Together we will raise strong, virtuous children.

6. Together we will be faithful to one another and exercise self-restraint.

7. Together we will remain lifelong partners.

When they return to their seats, the bride will move to sit on the groom's left side, taking the closest possible position to his heart. The groom then offers the bride a sacred necklace around her neck, and applies red vermillion powder to the crown of her forehead. These two offerings signify the bride's status as a married woman and the groom's devotion to the bride. They exchange rings at this time, and feed each other sweets.

—— JAPANESE SANSANKUDO, A SAKE RITUAL ——

YOU: From ancient times, drinking from the same cup has symbolized the strongest of bonds into which two people can enter: a powerful symbol of agreement, of affection, and of peace. Sipping from the same cup symbolizes the life the couple will share, each giving to the other generously and freely, each receiving from the other fully. This tradition is common to many cultures. The Japanese version of this ritual is called *sansankudo*, which means three times three, or nine, and signifies the concept of forever. Hikado and Audrey have adapted this ancient ritual for their wedding. On the table before us are three vessels of increasing size. I will pour three portions of sake into each cup, and Audrey and Hikado will each sip three times from each cup. May the sharing of these cups symbolize the sharing of your life together. *The three wine cups are nested one inside the other. The celebrant pours three portions of sake into the smallest cup. The groom takes the cup, holds it for the bride, who sips three times. She holds the cup while the groom sips three times. The celebrant pours sake into the next larger cup, and the couple repeats the ritual. Again, the celebrant pours sake into the largest cup, and the couple drinks again. All is done silently.*

—— JEWISH WEDDING ELEMENTS ——

Circling

Historically, the bride circles her groom. Here is a modern variant.

YOU: A moment ago, when Lauren circled Anthony three times, Anthony circled Lauren three times, and then they both circled each other once, they were honoring an ancient Jewish tradition. In their interpretation, they circled each other to recognize the equal roles they play in their relationship and the unique qualities that each offers the other. In Jewish mysticism, the number seven represents the creative process, the number of times the earth rotated on its axis during its creation. Lauren and Anthony circled each other seven times to demonstrate the priority and protection they will provide each other in their new shared life.

The Chuppah

YOU: We are holding this celebration underneath a canopy called a chuppah. *Chuppah* literally means that which covers or floats above. In Jewish custom, the chuppah is the house of promises; it is the home of hope. It represents the new home that Robert and Keiko are creating today.

The fact that the chuppah is open on all sides represents the ideal of hospitality: Visitors will always know that this new home is open, ready to welcome them as honored guests. The chuppah is a rather fragile structure. It needs loving friends and family to hold it up, and this fact, too, is symbolic, for the real value of a home is not its framework: Its real value lies with the people who love and choose to be in it together as a family.

Breaking the Glass

YOU: To conclude our ceremony, we observe a Jewish custom—the breaking of the wine glass.

The shattering of this glass symbolizes that what matters most in life is the spirit, not the letter; the wine, not the cup. It also represents the uniqueness of the moment, for only Max and Matzi will sip from this glass—no others ever will. And it symbolizes that our joy in this union is so great that no vessel can contain it. May this marriage be blissful until this glass is whole again! As Max steps on the glass, you may shout, *"Mazel Tov"* (Congratulations).

Note: If you are asked to provide a wine glass for crushing, it helps to slip the glass into an athletic sock before wrapping it in a large napkin. When the glass is crushed, the sock does wonders to keep in all the shards. I have heard of some officiants providing pre-wrapped light bulbs, which crush easily, but a good stomp will demolish most glasses—just look for thin glass.

JUMPING THE BROOM
(African, European, and Celtic Traditions)

The custom of marrying over a *besom*, or flowering branch, originated among Romani Gypsies in Wales and England. Meanwhile, in Ghana, West Africa, cleansing brooms were waved above the heads of newlyweds and their parents to chase away bad spirits. The custom of jumping the broom grew in America among some slaves as a way to marry amidst a punitive culture that forbade slave marriages. The custom ebbed away after the emancipation. In the 1970s, the novel and televised miniseries *Roots* popularized jumping the broom, as it appealed to wide audiences. Some Wiccans have also adopted the practice. The couple can simply step over a decorated or new broom as they recess, without comment. Alternatively:

YOU: Jumping the broom is an old tradition. The wedding couple used a brightly decorated broom to sweep out the old and to jump into their new lives. The ritual represents the joining of the couple, the combining of two families, and the need for the community to support their marriage. It also demonstrates the couple's determination to leap over obstacles—together—as they embark upon their future.

(Grandmother or mother), will you please bring the broom to us? *Grandmother or mother places the broom in front of the groom and bride.*

Will you all please now join me in counting to three for them to jump. All together now: one, two, three! *The couple joins hands and jumps over the broom together.*

NATIVE AMERICAN WEDDING ELEMENTS

Hand Washing

Native American culture comprises many tribes, each holding distinct traditions and customs. One tradition common to many tribes is the washing of hands.

YOU: Water symbolizes purification and cleansing. The bride and groom will now partake in a ceremonial washing of hands to wash away their past, good and bad, old deeds and previous lovers, so they can start their marriage fresh. *Pick up a small pitcher and slowly pour a little water over their hands. Hold a bowl beneath their hands. Provide a small towel for them to dry off.*

Blue and White Blankets (Cherokee)

Cover the bride's shoulders with a blue blanket, and do the same for the groom. Later, after the vows, remove the blue blankets and place one white blanket over the shoulders of the couple. This moment begins their married life.

─── PERSIAN WEDDING ELEMENTS ───

Gaining Consent

YOU: In this ritual, we establish that both parties are here of their own free will. This is especially important for the bride to affirm, and she is given just three chances to confirm or to silently decline the marriage proposal, with the help of her family.

Please listen carefully for her answer.

First, I ask the groom. Arthur, are you ready to enter into this contract of marriage, of your own free will?

ARTHUR: Yes.

YOU: Mojgan, are you ready to enter into this contract of marriage, of your own free will?

FRIEND #1: No, she is not ready; she still has cooking classes to take!

YOU: Mojgan, I ask for the second time, are you ready to enter into this contract of marriage, of your own free will?

FRIEND #2: No, she is not ready; she has too many suitors to choose from!

YOU: I will ask one last time. Mojgan, are you ready to enter into this contract of marriage, of your own free will?

MOJGAN: Yes!

YOU: Whew, that was close. Now we can proceed.

Honey Tasting

YOU: Our ceremony this afternoon includes an ancient Persian ritual. Mark and Rowena now symbolize the sharing of their lives, their promise to nurture each other and their intention to speak sweetly to one another by feeding each other from a cup of honey. *They dip their pinkies in honey and feed each other.*

An alternative honey ritual:

YOU: Hamid and Rebecca will now symbolize their intention to always speak sweetly to one another, and to have only agreeable and amiable words when they speak about each other. This is represented by dipping their fingers into a cup of honey and giving each other a taste of the sweetness.

Sofreh ye Aghd

YOU: Here we see Parviz and Azadeh seated before the *Sofreh ye Aghd*, which is an ancient Persian wedding tradition. *Aghd* refers to the legal process of getting married and signing the contract. And the *sofreh* is a spread before them filled with a number of ritualistic decorations, each symbolizing good wishes and blessings for the couple.

For example, the mirror, in which the bride and groom see their reflection, represents brightness in their future, while the lit candelabras on each side of the mirror represent light and energy. There are also eggs and almonds for fertility, flowers for beauty, honey for sweetness, and gold coins for abundance.

Sugar Ritual

YOU: I ask the couple's sisters and cherished women friends and family to come forward.

During this service, these women will hold a fine white cloth over the couple's head. The women will rub two sugar cones over the cloth, sprinkling sweetness over their union. This action represents their wishes that goodness, kindness, and gentleness will permeate throughout Rebecca and Hamid's marriage, their life together, and the family they will create. *The women begin rubbing the sugar cones, and stop after the marriage address.*

chapter nine

SELECTED PROSE AND POETRY FOR READINGS

What follows is a deliberately spare selection of wedding readings gathered with an eye toward what is most unusual and interesting.

You will find a huge number of additional readings in older wedding books and online (see Further Reading, page 128, for some good places to start), including pieces written by:

- Shakespeare
- Kahlil Gibran
- Pablo Neruda
- Elizabeth Barrett Browning
- Maya Angelou
- Wendell Berry
- Scriptural poets of all religions

ROMANTIC AND PHILOSOPHICAL READINGS

Excerpt from "Any husband or wife"
by Carol Haynes

Let us be guests in one another's house
With deferential "No" and courteous "Yes";
Let us take care to hide our foolish moods
Behind a certain show of cheerfulness.

Let us avoid all sullen silences;
We should find fresh and sprightly things to say;
I must be fearful lest you find me dull,
And you must dread to bore me any way.

Let us knock gently at each other's heart,
Glad of a chance to look within—and yet
Let us remember that to force one's way
Is the unpardoned breach of etiquette.

So shall I be hostess—you, the host—
Until all need for entertainment ends;
We shall be lovers when the last door shuts,
But what is better still—we shall be friends.

The Art of Marriage
by Wilferd A. Peterson

The little things are the big things.
It is never being too old to hold hands.
It is remembering to say "I love you" at least once a day.

It is never going to sleep angry.
It is at no time taking the other for granted;
the courtship should not end with the honeymoon,
it should continue through all the years.

It is having a mutual sense of values and common objectives.
It is standing together facing the world.
It is forming a circle of love that gathers in the whole family.
It is doing things for each other, not in the attitude of duty or
    sacrifice,
but in the spirit of joy.

It is speaking words of appreciation and demonstrating
    gratitude in thoughtful ways.
It is not expecting the husband to wear a halo or the wife to have
    wings of an angel.
It is not looking for perfection in each other.

It is cultivating flexibility, patience, understanding, and a sense
    of humor.
It is having the capacity to forgive and forget.
It is giving each other an atmosphere in which each can grow.

It is finding room for the things of the spirit.
It is a common search for the good and the beautiful.
It is establishing a relationship in which the independence is equal,
dependence is mutual and the obligation is reciprocal.
It is not only marrying the right partner, it is being the right partner.

Comfort Together

by Dinah Maria Craik

Oh the comfort—
the inexpressible comfort of feeling safe with a person,
having neither to weigh thoughts nor measure words,
but pouring them all right out
just as they are
chaff and grain together,
certain that a faithful hand will take and sift them—
keep what is worth keeping,
and then with the breath of kindness blow the rest away.

Excerpt from "Reflections on Marriage"

by Daphne Rose Kingma, from Weddings from the Heart

In marriage we say not only, "I love you today," but also "I promise to love you tomorrow, the next day, and always."

In promising always, we promise each other time. We promise to exercise our love, to stretch it large enough to embrace the unforeseen realities of our future. We promise to learn to love beyond the level of our instincts and inclinations, to love in foul weather as well as good, to love in hard times as well as when we are exhilarated by the pleasures of romance.

We change because of these promises. We shape ourselves according to them; we live in their midst and live differently because of them. We feel protected because of them. Our souls are protected; our hearts have come home.

This Marriage
by Rumi, translated by Coleman Barks

This marriage be wine with halvah, honey dissolving in milk.
This marriage be the leaves and fruit of a date tree.
This marriage be women laughing together for days on end.
This marriage, a sign to study.
This marriage, beauty.
This marriage, a moon in a light blue sky.
This marriage, this silence fully mixed with spirit.

Excerpts from "Song of the Open Road"
by Walt Whitman

Listen! I will be honest with you
I do not offer the old smooth prizes, but offer rough new prizes.
These are the days that must happen to you:
You shall not heap up what is called riches,
You shall scatter with lavish hand all that you earn or achieve.

Afoot and lighthearted, take to the open road,
Healthy, free, the world before you,
The long brown path before you leading wherever you choose.

Camerado, I give you my hand!
I give you my love more precious than money,
I give you myself before preaching or law;
Will you give me yourself? Will you come travel with me?
Shall we stick by each other as long as we live?

To My Dear and Loving Husband
by Anne Bradstreet

If ever two were one, then surely we.
If ever man were lov'd by wife, then thee.
If ever wife was happy in a man,
Compare with me, ye women, if you can.
I prize thy love more than the whole Mines of gold
Or all the riches that the East doth hold,
My love is such that Rivers cannot quench,
Nor ought but love from thee, give recompense.
Thy love is such I can no way repay.
The heavens reward thee manifold, I pray.
Then while we live, in love let's so presever
That when we live no more, we may live ever.

CULTURE-SPECIFIC READINGS

An American Blessing

This popular blessing has long been attributed to Apaches, Navajos, and other Native Americans. It was actually adapted from the script of an American Western movie in 1950 called Broken Arrow, *starring James Stewart and Debra Paget. Even with its Hollywood history, it remains a folkloric American poem.*

Now you will feel no rain,
for each of you will be a shelter to the other;
Now you will feel no cold,
for each of you will be warmth to the other;
Now there is no more loneliness,
for each of you will be companion to the other;
Now you are two bodies,
but there is only one life before you.
Go now to your dwelling place
and enter into your togetherness,
and may your days be good and long upon the earth!

Bahá'í

Excerpts from "The Marriage Tablet"
by Abdu'l-Bahá

The bond that unites hearts most perfectly is loyalty.

Allow no trace of jealousy to creep between you, for jealousy, like unto poison, vitiates the very essence of love. Let not the ephemeral incidents and accidents of this changeful life cause a rift between you. When differences present themselves, take counsel together in secret, lest others magnify a speck into a mountain. Harbor not in your hearts any grievance, but rather explain its nature to each other with such frankness and understanding that it will disappear, leaving no remembrance.

Your thoughts must be lofty, your ideals luminous, your minds spiritual, so that your souls may become a dawning-place for the Sun of Reality. Let your hearts be like unto two pure mirrors reflecting the stars of the heaven of love and beauty.

Together make mention of noble aspirations and heavenly concepts. Let there be no secrets one from another. Make your home a haven of rest and peace. Be hospitable, and let the doors of your house be open to the faces of friends and strangers. Welcome every guest with radiant grace and let each feel that it is his own home.

Lay the foundation of your affection in the very center of your spiritual being, at the very heart of your consciousness, and let it not be shaken by adverse winds.

And, when God gives you sweet and lovely children, consecrate yourselves to their instruction and guidance, so that they may become imperishable flowers of the divine rose-garden, nightingales of the ideal paradise, servants of the world of humanity, and the fruit of the tree of your life.

Buddhist

Excerpts from a Buddhist Marriage Homily
author unknown

In the future, happy occasions will come as surely as the morning.
Difficult times will come as surely as the night.
When things go joyously, meditate according to the Buddhist
   tradition.
When things go badly, meditate.
Meditation in the manner of the Compassionate Buddha will
   guide your life.
To say the words "love and compassion" is easy.
But to accept that love and compassion are built upon patience
   and perseverance is not easy.
Your marriage will be firm and lasting if you remember this.

Chinese Proverbs and Poems

May the petals of your lives as individuals become the soil that
   nurtures the flower of your new life together.

May you always know what is in each other's heart, for that
   unspoken bond allows your two hearts to beat as one, like the
   two wings of the Phoenix.

May your inner light always shine for your beloved. As the stars
   and the moon brighten the night sky, so too may your shared
   light brighten the lives of others.

May your lives on earth grow strong from one root. May your
   lives in heaven soar high on one wing.

Married Love
by Kuan Tao-Sheng, translated from the Chinese by Kenneth Rexroth and Ling Chung

You and I have so much love
That it burns like a fire,
In which we bake a lump of clay
Molded into a figure of you
And a figure of me.
Then we take both of them,
And break them into pieces,
And mix the pieces with water,
And mold again a figure of you,
And a figure of me.
I am in your clay.
You are in my clay.
In life we share a single quilt.
In death we will share one bed.

A Traditional Chinese Poem
Anonymous author, first century BCE

I want to be your friend
forever and ever.
When the hills are all flat
and the rivers are all dry,
when the trees blossom in winter
and the snow falls in summer,
when heaven and earth mix—not 'til then will I part from you.

An Inuit Traditional Love Song

You are my husband (wife).
My feet run because of you,
My feet dance because of you,
My heart beats because of you,
My eyes see because of you,
My mind thinks because of you,
And I shall love because of you.

Jewish

Seven Blessings *(Sheva Brachot)*

Seven blessings are traditionally recited during a Jewish wedding, after a couple shares vows and exchanges rings. Here are excerpts from five of the traditional blessings:

Blessed are You, Holy One of the Earth, who creates the fruit of the vine.

Blessed are You, Holy One of the Universe. You created all things for your Glory.

Blessed are You, Holy One of the World. Through you mankind lives.

Blessed are You, Holy One of the Cosmos, who gladdens this couple.

Blessed are You, Holy One of All, who created joy and gladness, loving couples, mirth, glad song, pleasure, delight, love, loving communities, peace, and companionship.

In a contemporary alternative, different guests present each of the following blessings, wishes, offerings, or gifts. For example, each member of the wedding party can read one.

FIRST GIFT GIVER: We bless this couple in the name of Friendship. (*Or* We offer this couple the gift of Friendship.) May this marriage prosper in the passing years with the strengthening bonds of two who know, trust, and savor each other.

SECOND GIFT GIVER: We bless this couple in the name of Intimacy. May this marriage discover the satisfaction of deep sharing.

THIRD GIFT GIVER: We bless this couple in the name of Justice. May this marriage seek what is fine and right, and flourish with love and respect.

FOURTH GIFT GIVER: We bless this couple in the name of Wisdom. May this marriage write a new chapter in the book of experience, husband and wife each learning from the other.

FIFTH GIFT GIVER: We bless this couple in the name of Joy. May this marriage hear the song of gladness, through word of mouth and meditation of heart.

SIXTH GIFT GIVER: We bless this couple in the name of Creativity. May this marriage create special dreams, and revel in their fulfillment.

SEVENTH GIFT GIVER: We bless this couple in the name of Appreciation. May this marriage flourish, as they keep their hearts open to each other, day and night.

EIGHTH GIFT GIVER: We bless this couple in the name of Kindness. May this marriage show that these two can treat each other always with generosity and good will.

You will find more sources for readings and rituals in the next chapter.

chapter ten

RESOURCES

FURTHER READING

These books and online resources help make it easy to craft meaningful wedding ceremonies.

CREATING A WEDDING SCRIPT

Basayne, Henry S., and Linda R. Janowitz. *Weddings: The Magic of Creating Your Own Ceremony* (Cupertino, CA: Happily Ever After Press, 2006).

Kingma, Daphne Rose. *Weddings from the Heart: Contemporary and Traditional Ceremonies for an Unforgettable Wedding* (York Beach, ME: Conari Press, 2002).

Reid, Dayna. *Sacred Ceremony: Create and Officiate Personalized Wedding Ceremonies* (Charleston, SC: CreateSpace, 2011).

The Ceremony Board at Wedding Bee.com hosts all kinds of questions, answers, and discussions about wedding ceremonies, including traditions from various faiths and cultures: ***www.weddingbee.com***

TheKnot.com has great information on wedding ceremonies; more than fifty links connect you with ideas for your ceremony, including Muslim, Mormon, Lutheran, Eastern Orthodox, and Humanist weddings: *wedding.theknot.com/ wedding-planning/wedding-ceremony.aspx*

DESTINATION WEDDINGS

Hotchkiss, Alison. *Destination Wedding Planner: The Ultimate Guide to Planning a Wedding from Afar* (San Francisco: Chronicle Books, 2009).

WEDDING VOWS AND READINGS

Hass, Robert, and Stephen Mitchell, eds. *Into the Garden, A Wedding Anthology: Poetry and Prose on Love and Marriage* (New York: Harper Perennial, 1994).

Nelson, Gertrud Mueller, and Christopher Witt. *A Wedding with Spirit: A Guide to Making Your Wedding (and Marriage) More Meaningful* (New York: Three Rivers Press, 2006).

Paris, Wendy, and Andrew Chesler. *Words for the Wedding: Creative Ideas for Personalizing Your Vows, Toasts, Invitations, and More* (New York: Perigee Trade, 2011).

Roney, Carley. *The Knot Guide to Wedding Vows and Traditions (Revised Edition): Readings, Rituals, Music, Dances, and Toasts* (New York: Potter Style, 2013).

The Poetry Foundation has a wonderful page of poetic possibilities for the wedding ceremony: *www.poetryfoundation.org/ article/178475*

AFRICAN AMERICAN WEDDING POETRY

Sturgis, Ingrid. *The Nubian Wedding Book: Words and Rituals to Celebrate and Plan an African-American Wedding* (New York: Three Rivers Press, 1998).

You can also find poetry here: *africanweddingtraditions.com/ african-american-love-poetry.html*

CHINESE, JAPANESE, AND KOREAN WEDDING CUSTOMS

Costa, Shu Shu. *Wild Geese and Tea: An Asian-American Wedding Planner* (New York: Riverhead Trade, 1998).

SAME-SEX WEDDINGS

It can be helpful to see how various couples handle choreography questions of the ancient, and in some ways archaic, wedding ceremony. **Gay Weddings.com** and **EquallyWed .com** are good places to start.

Touissant, David, and Heather Leo. *Gay and Lesbian Weddings: Planning the Perfect Same-Sex Ceremony* (New York: Ballantine Books, 2004).

JEWISH WEDDING RITUALS AND CUSTOMS

Diamant, Anita. *The New Jewish Wedding, Revised* (New York: Scribner, 2001).

INTERCULTURAL AND INTERFAITH

Macomb, Rev. Susanna Stefanachi, and Andrea Thompson. *Joining Hands and Hearts: Interfaith, Intercultural Wedding Celebrations* (New York: Fireside, 2003).

PROPS

Most often, the bride and groom will furnish their own props, such as the Unity candle or the sand and appropriate containers. They should also bring their own wine and glasses for the wine ceremony. You would be wise, however, to provide the following as needed:

* Matches or a lighter for a candle ceremony
* A small decorative dish and local honey for a honey ceremony
* A length of ribbon for handfasting (try fabric and floral shops)
* A back-up bottle opener for a wine ceremony
* A wine glass and large fabric napkin for the glass-breaking ceremony (consignment or thrift shops are good for this)

ROBES

Murphy Robes is an excellent provider of clergy, judicial, and choir robes: *www.murphyrobes.com*. Check online for other stores. Consider getting lightly used robes at local thrift shops or on **eBay.com**. Or rent one. A white robe exudes a church-like or choir-like feeling, while a black robe looks judicial. Craft fairs and boutiques are good sources for robes and flowing jackets that can feel fancy, festive, and appropriate.

STOLES

A stole is a thin cloth that some officiants wear around their necks. It's a further delineation of the role you play, so you can't be confused with the catering staff. Many stoles have Christian emblems, but you can also, sometimes, find stoles that have abstract designs or non-denominational symbols.

I've found reversible stoles in my local Christian-goods store; they have a cross on one side and plain fabric on the other. Also try **eBay.com** and **etsy.com**. Stoles can be expensive. An organization called Justices of the Peace of the U.S. sells monogrammed stoles starting at $64 (**jpus.org/stoles.htm**). Consider asking a seamstress or tailor to whip one up for you.

NOTES

Much of the content I've used comes from my own wedding experience and from training with my father. The remarks from new officiants and wedding coordinators were gathered from personal interviews.

CHAPTER ONE

"The Civil or Secular Ceremony." Percentages were according to surveys conducted by the Pew Research Center for the People and the Press: *www.pewforum.org/unaffiliated /nones-on-the-rise.aspx*

CHAPTER TWO

Read much more about marriage licenses and their evolution in America in the *Legislative Guide to Marriage Law* (2005) at *www.legis .iowa.gov/DOCS/Central /Guides/marriage.pdf*

The John Arthur story is from "Ohio Gay Couple Wins Right to be Buried Together" by Jennifer Lai, Slate, June 24, 2013.

You can also read more about Chris Reimer's wedding at this blog post: *www.rizzotees.com/blog /performing-a-wedding-ceremony -is-a-thrill-and-honor*

CHAPTER EIGHT

The passage recited during the candle ceremony is attributed to Rabbi Yisroel ben Eliezer, often called Baal Shem Tov, or Besht. A Jewish mystical rabbi, he is considered to be the founder of Hasidic Judaism.

CHAPTER NINE

"Oh the comfort" [Comfort Together]. These lines occur in Chapter 16 of Craik's 1859 novel, *A Life for a Life*. London: Collins' Clear Type Press, 1900.

The history behind "Apache Wedding Song" [An American Blessing] came from Rebecca Mead's book, *One Perfect Day: The Selling of the American Wedding*, p. 135. New York: Penguin, 2007.

PERMISSIONS/CREDITS

ACKNOWLEDGMENTS

So many smart and helpful people contributed to this book. Alison Hotchkiss listened to my ideas over a latte at Caffe Trieste and kindly introduced me to her editor. For this native San Franciscan, writing something for Chronicle Books has been a lifelong dream. Chronicle editors Lisa Tauber and Dawn Yanagihara believed in and improved this book, and the Chronicle team—designer Hillary Caudle; managing editors Doug Ogan, Marie Oishi, and Elizabeth Smith; and production manager Steve Kim—graciously ushered me through the publishing process. In addition, Doris Ober helped to develop my original soup of ideas into the book over a long winter. Michael Basayne, Debra Carpenter, Susan deQuattro, Jacqueline Doyle, Jennifer Randolph, and Jenny Walicek read drafts, offered encouragement, helped me to stay organized, and stimulated new epiphanies. Thank you to all the new officiants and experienced wedding planners whose interviews in these pages made the book more useful and fun. Gratitude to my wedding clients and colleagues who taught and inspired me with beautiful and nontraditional weddings. And a special thank you to my husband, Mark Baumann, for so much.